The Journey of a Lifetime

DR. J. SHERMAN PELT

DEDICATION

This book is dedicated to Dr. J. Sherman Pelt's Father, Mr. John Sherman Pelt, Jr. and Mother, Mrs. Addie Montgomery Pelt, whom he loved dearly, as well as, his devoted Grandfather (Gramps), Mr. George Montgomery, who took on the role of father after his father passed.

This book is also dedicated to Dr. Pelt's beloved deceased siblings, Juanita Pelt Winters, George Pelt, Sr. and Evonne Pelt.

Additionally, this book is dedicated to the parishioners and former parishioners of Bethlehem Baptist Church – Boligee, Alabama, Hill First Baptist Church – Athens, Georgia and Liberty Baptist Church – Atlanta, Georgia, the three churches where Dr. Pelt served as Senior Pastor.

INVITATION

In this book, Dr. J. Sherman Pelt invites you to join him as he traces his life's history. In his own words, "The invitation is given so that you may see the hand of God working on and through a person who is weak, and how God continues to lift him up and plant his feet on solid ground." In October 2013, Dr. Pelt transitioned from his earthly journey to his heavenly home. He began the writing of this work and it was completed by his family, in accordance with his request.

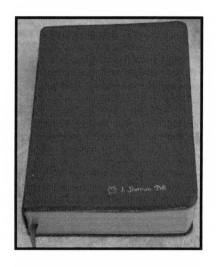

CONTENTS

FORWARD

My brother, Dr. John Sherman Pelt, was better known to us as Sherman. Sherman and I were close not only in age (fifteen- and one-half months apart), but as a brother, friend, classmate and sounding board. Writing this endorsement is both difficult and a great pleasure because of the importance of sharing his life story with others. This book gives some insight into growing up in rural Alabama. We grew up in a four-room house, with no running water and an outhouse. Three of us boys slept in the same bed. I remember well what Sherman describes regarding the conditions black people experienced living in Alabama during those times. Separation by race was a standard practice, but we survived; because we can do all things by the grace of God.

Growing up, we observed that there was something different about Sherman. We didn't quite understand it at the time; however, God had placed a special calling on his life. He was set apart to preach, teach and spread the love of God. I remember like yesterday when he told us that he had been called to the ministry. After telling Gramps and our mother what the Lord had called him to do, he and I went outside in the yard, I asked him "are you sure?" He told me, "yes!" I then said, "I can't believe you are going to become a preacher." His reply was, "You got to do what God tells you to do." Some years later, I was serving in the military, I went to visit him and his beautiful wife Mary in Huntsville, Alabama; I remember him repeating those same words to me. He was a Shoe Store Manager; Mary had an outstanding job with NASA/Marshall Space Flight Center and they had recently purchased a new home. When he shared with me that he had been told by God to go to seminary in

Atlanta and they would be moving, I asked, "why are you giving all of this up to move to a one room apartment?" He said, "You just don't understand, you got to do what God tells you to do." What he was saying to me was to let God lead your life and you follow. If you do this you will be successful in life, and you will have God's favor. As he neared the end of his life, he said, "If the Lord heals my body or take my spirit to live with Him forever, either way I win!"

Raymond Pelt, Sr.
Brother of Dr. J. Sherman Pelt

Forward

My brother, Sherman gained the respect of all those who knew him. During our childhood, I remember a time when he seldom talked to anyone except our brother Raymond and I. Everyone else just got a few words and that was it. When asked why he didn't talk like everyone else, he said he didn't have a reason to talk. Our mother would always try to make him talk. The more she pressured him, the less he talked. One day, I went into the kitchen of that old house we rented as sharecroppers, where our mother was standing in front of the open window, washing a big pan of dishes. As I began to talk to her, she put her hand to her lips signaling me to be quiet. She pointed to the window. I heard Raymond and Sherman playing, talking and laughing. Sherman was making most of the noise and doing most of the talking. Anyone who knew our mother knew she had a temper. She said, "that little Rascal can talk to everybody but me." To say that our mother was not happy with him would be an understatement. She called Sherman to the back door and told me to go play. I don't know what was used, but I do know, Mama didn't spare the rod that day. Sherman quickly became very talkative in the following days.

Our grandfather (Gramps) prided himself as being the best fruit and vegetable Businessman in the area. One day, he asked Sherman and I to deliver two dozen ears of corn, a cantaloupe, and one of his prized watermelons to an elderly white couple that lived in a huge plantation style mansion a few miles from our house. We loaded the old 1960 Chevy Apache 10 pickup and headed out. Imagine us driving up to a house with big white columns that reached from the porch to the 2nd floor roof. As we pulled into the driveway, we were confused as to where to park. Sherman was driving and he stopped directly in front of the house. We carried the items in our arms to the front door. After several times knocking on the huge door, I saw movement and the curtain of a side window to the door opened. The elderly lady just stared at us for about five seconds and walked away. Sherman knocked again. She then called her husband to come to the door. In the midst of Sherman saying we were there to deliver the items; she said to her husband, "There's a Darky at the door. There's a Darky at the door." The elderly man approached the window and yelled, "You can't come to my front door; you need to go around to the back." After saying that, he immediately closed the curtain. Sherman looked at me and said, "Let's leave it on the front porch; I'm not going to the back." A few hours later, Gramps returned home very angry with us. He accused us of "ruining his business and the respect he had spent years to gain." He said we had to go back and apologize. Without hesitation, Sherman said, "I'm not going back." Our Mother agreed we did the right thing and said we did not have to go back. Needless to say, things at the house were tense for a few days, but that day I gained total respect for my brother Sherman and that day he became MY HERO. Years later, he considered buying that house and operating it as a Bed & Breakfast.

Nathaniel Pelt
Brother of Dr. J. Sherman Pelt

FORWARD

As the youngest child, I have always loved and admired my big brother, Sherman. A few people called him John and his nickname as a child was Pony. Growing up, I remember those farm chores; working in the fields, picking peas, pulling watermelons, etc.

While attending J. F. Drake State Community & Technical College in Huntsville, Alabama, I lived with Sherman and his wife, Mary, for several months. I enjoyed the time spent with them because we all got along well. Sherman was fun to be around and we shared a lot of laughs. Sherman and Mary moved to Atlanta and after working for a period of time in Birmingham, I moved back home to Eutaw in Greene County, Alabama. He was always a supportive and caring brother. After Sherman and his family moved to Georgia, he always found time to come to my home and visit with me and my family. Down through the years, we stayed in close contact with one another.

As a youth and as an adult, I looked up to him as a great big brother, a child of God, and a Minister of the Gospel. I think of him every day and will always miss him. However, God knows best; He is in control of the time we have on this earth.

Fredrick Pelt, Sr.
Brother of Dr. J. Sherman Pelt

PREFACE

The Holy Spirit gave my beloved husband peace about his condition; therefore, I received peace from the way he accepted his illness. God gave him strength and I was strengthened by and through his strength. The thought of losing my soulmate, my best friend, my husband was utterly devastating and I honestly did not know how I would survive it – but GOD! Many around me - family, friends and others, thought I would lose it – but GOD! I'm still here and doing those things God would have me to do only by His grace, mercy and peace! Fervent prayer, Scripture reading and meditation were essential to my ability to keep moving. God gave me the strength in many ways and through many others down through the years, by their teachings, examples, cards, calls, visits, love and support. The enormous love and support of our children was priceless! Opportunities to speak publicly about my loss at Liberty and other venues on numerous occasions assisted greatly with the grieving process.

To God be the glory for all He has done, is doing, and will do!

- Mary O. Pelt

Acknowledgements

First and foremost, I give God the praise, the honor and the glory for being able to complete this book. It was God who gave me the strength to finish the work started by my beloved late husband seven years ago. Without Him I can do nothing, but with Him I can do all things through Christ.

In addition, gratitude is expressed to all who assisted, in any way, with the publication of this book. The enthusiastic willingness by my brothers-in-law Raymond, Nathaniel and Fredrick Pelt, to read and provide invaluable information regarding specific events is also greatly appreciated. Special thanks to our children, Tyrone & Cherline and Nicklaus & Chailoea for your love, support and contributions to the completion of this work left to us by your father. You all are truly a blessing from God. Your prayers, words of wisdom, encouragement, editing, proofreading, text formatting, layout, cover design, and all other acts of support are greatly appreciated.

- Mary O. Pelt

INTRODUCTION

The Biblical and theological construct that have shaped my perspective of life is Romans 8:28. It states, "And we know that all things work together for good to them that love God, to them who are the called according to His purpose." (KJV) This text confirms for me that the complexities that we find in our reality have a purpose in the scheme of things; and somehow, God merges the varieties, the differences into a system that functions to produce the desired result. God processes the bad and good, the desired and the undesirable into something worthwhile.

"All things," is an all-inclusive statement embracing everything that can be considered. Things that are pleasant and unpleasant; and things that are positive and negative. This is a sweeping statement that does not filter anything out of the trash from the primary thing.

This idea of "all things" reminds me of my mother making quilts for the winter. She would get all of the old clothes that she could find; shirts, pants, coats, etc. The clothes would be different colors, textures, designs, and qualities. My mother would systematically cut the clothes into smaller pieces. Then, she would sew the pieces together in a specific order until one side of the quilt was finished. She would do the same to make the other side. With the assistance of others, she would place a layer of cotton in the center and sew the two sides together. Voilà, there you have a creatively designed warm quilt to keep you warm throughout the winter.

If my mother could get a variety of fabrics, colors, designs and textures of cloth to make a warm beautiful quilt, I can comprehend how Paul can write, "all things work together for the good." My mother was not the only person in her day, who knew the art of quilting; there were others who had been taught this art of taking what was worn out, out of style, no longer useful, and creating a new, beautiful thing. If my mother and others could make quilts, God surely knows how to put the different pieces of reality together and create something significant, meaningful and important.

Paul is specifically saying that the believer does not have to be concerned with things running in different directions because it will come together and serve its purpose. This statement is for "those who love The Lord." This affirms to me that I am also considered in this statement. Regardless of what I encounter, what I have to face, it will work out for my good. This concept is major for me. During the difficult task of pastoral ministry for thirty-two (32) years, I have used this as a foundational principle to keep a positive attitude through difficult situations. I have used this mindset in all of life situations.

When I hear people talking about the glass that is filled to its midpoint, debating the proverbial question, whether the glass is half empty, or half full, I have a different perspective. But if I am forced to keep strictly with the question, my answer would be that it is half full. Nevertheless, my original answer is that the glass fully contains God's blessing to quench a person's thirst. I am more excited there is water in the cup; enough to drink and be refreshed. A half glass of water is significant enough to help to hydrate the body. If we label that amount half empty or half full, it will not make it less or more.

By having a positive perspective on life, where "all things work together for the good," when I discovered that I had Multiple

Myeloma, I still had a positive view of life although the initial news was shocking and life changing. However, after the reality had settled in and I got my balance, I was focused on living my life to the end serving God, no matter what. I accepted the possibility of dying earlier than I had expected. After all, we do not know when death will make that proverbial knock at our door. It is important to be prepared when the knock is made.

Most importantly, as I processed my situation, I felt that God allowed this to happen to me to squeeze the best out of me and deepen my spirituality. I already was a positive person but this made me even more positive on the outlook of life. The Holy Spirit gave me another anointing, where I became more in tune with Christ. I was already tuned in to the Word and will of Christ before this new revelation was given; but this increased the intensity of my spiritual connection. While traveling by automobile, listening to a FM or AM radio station the reception gets weaker as you get further from the station. On the other hand, the reception gets stronger as you get closer. The cancer ordeal caused me to travel closer to my spiritual station, and because I was driving in the direction of my power base, the voice of the Divine continued to get clearer. I am not attempting to suggest that I have arrived at the station; but I am saying that I am on my way.

This journey with the Lord is revealing to me that my early life in rural Alabama was a major part of my development to effectively engage in the ministry and challenges of life that I would face in my future. In the difficult days of me growing up, racism was not concealed at all. It was an everyday practice. Blacks worked hard on the plantations for half of what they produced. The white plantation owner got the other half just because he owned the land. My grandfather worked under this system, and we helped him work the farm. It was difficult to learn much when we were working the farm on many of the days that we should have been in school. In fact, I repeated the fourth grade. But I learned that if a person could live under those conditions and survive, that person can endure almost anything.

When things started to change for the best during my early teenage years, I felt that I could face anything. While facing difficult situations, I have often reminded myself that if I survived plowing a mule all day, picking cotton all day, chopping corn all day in the hot scorching sun, then I can succeed in anything. I can take on whatever comes my way.

With a strong faith in God and a background that shaped me to endure harshness and hardship with a smile, I concluded that I was the right one to model Christ to the world, while being challenged with cancer. Pastors have problems, we have issues, and we have health challenges, too. Where the rubber hits the road is, how am I going to respond to this condition? Will my faith stay intact? After preaching that God is a loving God for forty years, do I still believe that when trouble comes to my own address?

In my case, my faith has gotten stronger and my vision has gotten clearer that "all things work together for the good" for those of us that trust in Him. God is using me now in ways that I could not have been used otherwise. I have shared my journey in preaching, in workshops, in meeting with cancer patients, in counseling cancer patients, in sharing my story with people who were seriously ill and in praying with people who were very sick. I had played most of these roles before as a pastor, but there has been a new anointing since the Holy Spirit has given me a fresh anointing.

I invite you to join me, as I attempt to trace my life's history from birth to the present. I am not asking you to journey with me because you're bored and need something to do to occupy your time. Nor am I asking you to join me because I have lived a noteworthy life. The invitation is given so that you may see the hand of God working on and through a person who is weak, and how God continues to lift him up and plant his feet on solid ground. God lifted him up out of the cotton fields. God lifted him up out of illiteracy; God lifted him up out of poverty and shame, and is lifting him up out of cancer a second time.

Chapter 1

My Early Days

I am inspired to write this book because of me wrestling with some major health issues in the last five years. By writing these words I am gaining new insights into myself, my family and my life struggles in general. I am hopeful that my sharing will strengthen, empower and encourage others who may be facing similar circumstances.

These reflections have caused me to remember the suffering, sickness and pain of the past that takes me back to rural Alabama during the mid-1950s. I was the third child to be born to Mr. John Sherman Pelt and Mrs. Addie Mary Montgomery Pelt, in Forkland, Alabama. Until I was five years old, we lived in that setting. We lived in a three-room house on my paternal grandfather's property. My father plowed a mule to cultivate his cotton and corn, and drove a pulpwood truck. He also worked in a small factory to help make ends meet. With a two-year college degree, my mother was able to teach in a two-room school.

Approximately during the same time (1959), my father and maternal grandmother became ill. My father was diagnosed with scleroderma; a severe hardening of the skin and other vital organs; and my grandmother was diagnosed with cancer. Needless to say, this was a trying time for our family. My father lived for eight years with his disease, staying for long periods of time at the Veteran's Administration (VA) Hospital in Tuskegee, Alabama; but from what I know, my grandmother's struggle with her illness was brief. She died in April of 1960.

Because of what was happening at the time; the death of my grandmother and the long stays of my father in the hospital, we (my mother & my siblings) moved in with my maternal grandfather, George Montgomery. He lived in Clinton, Alabama, just twenty miles away. However, at the time it seemed a world away.

This situation was challenging for everyone. Naturally, my mother supported her father and mother, during the illness and death of her mother. Further, she felt that she could not abandon her grieving father. At the same time, her husband's (my father) life was predicted to be very short. Therefore, she did not have much of a future where she was. So, we relocated to Clinton.

It was one thing to visit my grandparents for Christmas a few days; but it became problematic taking up residence. For example, when my father was not in the hospital, he did not have a comfortable place to stay; several of us slept in one bed; our mother went from being a school teacher to a farm hand; our view of our granddaddy shifted to the left; and I believe his did the same because we got on his last nerve. This is not to say that there was not love in the house; but there were many other matters being worked out in the midst.

Yes, my grandfather was a sharecropper. He worked and managed a large farm with cattle, hogs, chickens, cotton, corn, and watermelons. He had peach and apple orchards, a large garden and grew a host of other things that one would find on a farm. He cultivated his farm with mule pulled plows and we removed the grass from the crop by chopping it with a hoe. Therefore, the work required intense manual labor.

My mother often told us stories about growing up on that farm as the only child; and worse than that, she was a girl. She said that she did a great job performing tasks that were considered men's jobs. Although they worked from "can to can't" (from sun up to sun down), because of the volume of work, my grandfather still had to employ people to help work the farm.

Although we were very young when we moved in with my grandfather, we represented an important part of the labor force that my grandfather needed years earlier. At the time, we were approximately between the ages of 2 and 8; with my older brother being 8, my sister 7, I was 5, my younger brother was 4; and my youngest brother at the time was 2. My youngest brother was born while we were living with my grandfather. We were assigned chores early in our stay in our new home. It was not long before my sister was cooking for the family using a wooden stove. According to our abilities, we played our part to help make things work. My brothers and I fed the chickens, the hogs, the cows, chopped cotton and corn, and plowed the fields. Life was difficult at that time.

Like so many farm families in the area, we missed many school days. If we attended school the first days of the school year, it was not long before we were out for several days. We often attended school on alternating days and rainy days. We attended school - "on again, off again." When the teachers called roll, the students would respond for the absent student by saying, "picking cotton." Then, the class would erupt in laughter. I was very sensitive to that habit of the class, because I knew that the same happened when I was out "picking cotton." Therefore, I was not quick to join in the laughter. During the planting (March & April) and harvesting (August, September & October) seasons, we often missed a week or two at a time. During the heavy cotton harvesting months, the rainy days assured that most of the school population was in attendance.

One had to make a major adjustment under these circumstances (being made fun of by the other children, not knowing the lesson assignments, being tired, alienated and etc.) to do well in school. The adjustments were overwhelming to me. When I did attend school, the adjustments were so overwhelming to me that it was impossible to learn anything. I was too tired to learn, I did not fit in and I saw my day in school as an off day from the sweltering heat; and the seemingly endless cotton rows.

In addition, I was a sickly child. I did not know it at the time, but I had allergies that were probably related to the plants and animals that I was constantly in contact with; I also had tonsillitis. When it got really bad, my mother took me to the doctor to get a penicillin shot. The doctor did not do much to determine the problem. This was an ongoing problem in my growing up. When I complained about not feeling well, my parents accused me of trying to get out of work.

During this time my father was very sick; and I felt that I could have had the same disease that he had. After all, my father's disease was never talked about, or explained to us. And when I went to the doctor, it was always said that I must have had a cold. In other words, it was not discussed, or at most, I was told, "you are always sick."

Actually, when I was told that I had Multiple Myeloma five years ago, I did a research of my father's disease; because to that point, I (we) did not know what my father died of. I discovered that it was scleroderma. At least I know now that I did not inherit my illness from my father.

My father died when I was 13 years old, and he was 55. It was on a beautiful fall day; October 25, 1968. This was my father's 55th birthday. But he was not feeling well because he had eaten some fresh pork that he was advised not to eat by his physician. In fact, he was on a very restricted diet because he had problems digesting food. But he vowed to eat some "fresh barbecued pork" if it killed him. It was not a spontaneous decision but a planned one.

My father purchased a pig and grew it to his ideal size. We killed it and cooked it according to my father's instructions and desire. Then, he ate until he was satisfied. He was very sick on Friday night and Saturday morning. My brother Raymond and I got up that Saturday morning, which was our father's birthday, and decided to earn some extra money by picking cotton for Mr. "Buck Jones." We usually finished harvesting our cotton the last of September of each year, and earned extra money by working for other people on Saturdays during October and the first weeks of November.

We were somewhat hesitant about leaving my father because he was sick, but my sister, Juanita and younger brothers, Nathaniel and Fredrick were there with him, and he said that he would be okay. Therefore, we spent the day picking cotton and having fun with other kids who were working with us. After we weighed the cotton and received payment for our work, we got on the back of the truck to go to the store. Just before we started to leave, my brothers Nathaniel and Fredrick came running through the woods to bring us the news that our father was dead. Exhausted, they got on the back of the truck with us and we proceeded on to the store because we had postponed lunch to finish what we were doing. I was going to get a pack of donuts. There were three large donuts in a pack. Of course, I lost my appetite, and I was ready to go home. When we finally got there the mortician was there collecting his body. It was a long night!

Because I craved donuts on the day of my father's death, it was several years before I could eat a donut again. Even to this day, I associate donuts with my father's death. Although we had always celebrated October 25th as my father's birthday, we discovered on the day of his death that his birth certificate recorded him as being born October 26th. This was a bitter sweet revelation. We were pleased that dad did not die on his birthday; but he had spent a lifetime celebrating his birthday on the wrong day.

A few years later, we moved into our own house only a few miles away from my grandfather. We continued the farm arrangement until I was a junior in high school. At that time, my mother and grandfather purchased a house together. The farming declined. We only farmed five or six acres, which consisted of watermelons, cantaloupes, sweet potatoes, peanuts, corn and field peas. We also had a large garden. We sold the produce in the surrounding area and to grocery stores in the nearby town.

At this point, we were able to attend school on a regular basis because we did not have the large cotton farm, which was approximately 20 acres and the corn which was about 10 acres. I played the trombone in the band and became involved in school activities. This is when I first really got excited about the learning process and decided that I wanted to go to college. Needless to say, I was a far cry from being prepared to take on such a venture because of my past academic record. I repeated the fourth grade and was a C student otherwise. Before the tenth grade, I did not have any interest in excelling academically. Therefore, during the last two years of high school, I spent a lot of time in the books trying to catch up on many of the things that I had missed over the years.

At the end of my junior year, I felt called/compelled to preach the Gospel, while knowing that I did not have the knowledge, courage, skills or background to take on this awesome task. After talking to my Pastor, Reverend Finest Gandy about my call, he strongly supported me. He tutored me intensively for several days to prepare me for my trial sermon on the afternoon of Father's Day in 1973. I confessed my call in May and preached in June. That was quick, and I was frightened in my boots. I had envisioned that I would start preaching after several months to one year.

My initial sermon went better than I had expected because of the loving support that I had from my family, church, community, classmates and friends. The sermon wasn't much; but the community support made it special. In writing this, I just realized that this event lifted my self-esteem for the rest of my life; because I didn't think that many people would come to hear 'little old me.' However, the church was filled with people who seemed to want me to succeed.

After the initial sermon, I had more preaching engagements than I could fill. I had no thought or dream that people knew me, to even invite me to their churches to preach. Since I had just turned eighteen years old, I was often invited by various local churches to be their Youth Day Preacher, or their Youth Revivalist. It really surprised me that things took off so fast. Although I was not prepared as a preacher, God used my weakness in a powerful way.

Chapter 2

Education, Family, Employment

I had a good senior year in high school. My grades improved and I became more of a part of the social scene. I was even elected senior class president. My call into the ministry had stimulated and motivated me to study, learn and reach out to others. Many of my classmates and teachers invited me to preach at their churches.

Prior to my call, I was in the marching band, but when I returned to school in my senior year I did not register for band. Actually, I had looked forward to playing first trombone because the person who held the position graduated the year before. I was next in line to carry on. However, I was not sure how this would fit my new life, and there were people close to me who felt the same way. As was the custom for the African American bands in that context and at that time, we were known to "get down". This is what drove my decision to discontinue something that I loved. The band teacher had tutored me to be ready for my senior year, and he was hopeful of getting me a band scholarship to his Alma Mater. He encouraged me to stay with the program, informing me of ministers who had graduated from band programs, and who were then band teachers. But I could not see myself being one of those people. I felt bad that I could not live up to his expectation by agreeing to stay in the band, but life moves on. With constant studying trying to improve my grades in general, and my communication skills in particular, the year passed swiftly. First hand, I discovered that reading with comprehension and writing with clarity were important. And I had to confess that I was very weak in both, but I committed myself to the task.

For one thing, I did not have much of a choice. I had to do a lot of Biblical study to prepare sermons, I had to write the sermons the best I could, so that the message that I preached made sense. I did not worry about the fire, the charisma, I had my share of that. I knew how badly I needed training to do this work, therefore, I greatly thirsted for and anticipated theological education. The people seemed to have loved my preaching, but I knew that I needed help in this area.

The senior prom came along, and I had another decision to make. Do I go to the prom? At that time and in that context, dancing and being a part of a party setting was viewed as not being a place for a preacher, young or old. But me and my high school sweetheart, Mary Outland, had looked forward to that occasion and we did go to the prom. It was a bit awkward at first. I wanted to dance or at least move to the music while sitting or walking around, but I felt that people were watching me. After being there for a while, I relaxed and enjoyed the evening. It was a memorable night.

We graduated from Paramount High School in Boligee, Alabama in May of 1974; my girlfriend, Mary Outland, attended Alabama A&M University in Huntsville, Alabama, and I decided to attend a small, approximately 700 students, Bible College with a big name, Selma University (a junior college of liberal arts degrees). The three basic degrees offered were an AA in General Education, a BA in Religion and a B.Th. in Theology. Many of the well-known African American preachers in the state of Alabama had attended this school. Therefore, my pastor and the Moderator of the local Mount Olive Missionary Baptist Association, who also studied there, felt that it was the only place for me.

I accepted my Pastor and Moderator's recommendation to attend Selma University. Like any other college freshman, I enjoyed the freedom of learning another world. It was a challenge getting up in time for those morning classes even using the alarm clock because I was going to bed later than usual. But once I adjusted the time that I went to bed, I was able to get to breakfast, lunch, dinner and class on time. It took more time to adjust to the teachers and classmates.

During the first few weeks of the first semester, there were announcements recruiting people to join the concert band. In a chapel service, those who had played in high school bands were asked to stand. Of course, I stood. Then, we were asked to remain in the chapel after worship. In that meeting, the band teacher reminded us that we were needed to keep the band in existence. He asked what instruments we played, and he also told us that a small scholarship came with the enrollment. Since I had not played in the band during my senior year in high school, I was inclined not to accept the offer; but I was the only person in the group that played the trombone. After being spoken to personally and asked to join the effort because of a need for at least one trombone in the band, I said yes and accepted the band director's offer.

There were about twenty-five (25) of us, in the concert band, if that many. We practiced a couple of times a week, during the evening. We played in chapel services and at special events. Although I did not possess any unusual skills in playing my instrument, it was satisfying being a part of the band.

I enjoyed my matriculation at Selma University. It was a Baptist School, where many of the state-wide meetings were held. I was able to meet and hear some of the leading Pastors, Lecturers and Preachers. We had chapel service Monday through Friday of each week; and attendance was mandatory.

During the time I attended Selma, there were approximately fifty ministers enrolled. We were a part of the Ministerial Alliance. This group was responsible for the Chapel services. It was established very much like a church, with the Ministerial Alliance President and Officers leading the group. The President often presided over the worship. The second year, I was elected to be the President of the Ministerial Alliance. Usually, the President was a mature pastor, who had enrolled in school at a late time in his life. Therefore, they knew the protocol of conducting the services. I had limited experience having been the pastor of a church for only one year. In other words, I accepted the position knowing that I was not qualified to hold the position. It took a considerable amount of time for me to plan for five services each week. However, the older pastors encouraged me and counseled me as I served. After a while, I felt somewhat at ease coming before that four to five hundred group each day. Of course, what made it even more difficult was the teachers were in attendance. Often, they would give their feedback regarding my presiding, or whatever role that I played in the worship that day.

Because of that exposure, I received many preaching opportunities at the school and at churches in the area. In addition, I received invitations from teachers and student pastors who lived in other areas. My Greek professor, a white Southern Baptist Preacher, talked to me concerning taking the standard approach to seminary, which was a regular BA or BS degree, maybe in Social Science, Political Science, Education, Biology, or History. Those were my stronger subjects. Then, do religious studies on the graduate level. One weekend my professor took me to the New Orleans Baptist Theological Seminary in New Orleans, Louisiana. We stayed in the home of a white family. The small child asked me, "why are you black?" The parents quickly stopped the child from speaking and apologized for his action. At another time, the child asked me, "how do you comb your hair?" His parents were not in the room that time, therefore, I got the pick out of my pocket and picked out my afro. He was amazed that I could comb my hair!

On that particular recruitment weekend, the school had a series of activities. We did a campus tour, Professors talked to us concerning their classes, we had chapel services, had lunch together and toured the city. This was a very informative weekend. Actually, it helped me to decide to complete the Associate of Arts degree (AA) at Selma and to pursue an Education degree at another college. I knew that I wanted to attend a Seminary; but I was sure that I would not attend the one that I had just visited. For one thing it was white, and it was obvious that they were attempting to recruit African Americans. Although they tried to be courteous, they did not have a clue to their insensitivities.

I graduated in May of 1976 from Selma University with an Associate of Arts (AA) Degree. During the summer, I stayed with my mother as I prepared to attend Livingston University in Livingston, Alabama (now the University of West Alabama) that fall. The school was just thirty-five (35) miles from my mother's home. I therefore commuted to school along with my preacher friend, The Reverend Arthur Coleman who had also transferred to Livingston University from Selma. He lived just eight miles away. He and I alternated in driving to the school. Another young man, Wesley also commuted with us. He did not have a car, but he supplied most of the gasoline for our travels.

The trips got to be very intense going and coming, because Wesley was a Jehovah's Witness, while Rev. Coleman and I were Baptist preachers. It seemed to have been Wesley's mission to correct us on Biblical doctrine. It got to a point that I told the group that I was not going to debate religion any more, and I didn't.

After the first semester, I started to look for a place on or near campus because the driving was too much for me. The commute did not allow adequate time for study at the library, or to be a part of the various study groups and school activities. I was able to find a boarding house with an old lady, Mrs. Lucy Jolly, who once lived about a mile from my mother's house. She was in her mid-eighties, and had a pretty little dog named Tricky. She talked to Tricky like she talked to me. However, I was glad to have a comfortable place to live and Mrs. Jolly was glad to have the son that she never had. I took her to the store, medical appointments, church and wherever she needed to go. We developed a mother and son relationship. She called me Preach, and I called her Mama Lucy. She would tell me stories of growing up as a black woman during the early 1900s.

Things had turned out well because Rev. Coleman got married and discontinued school and Wesley made other arrangements to continue his studies. Since Mama Lucy's house was only approximately three miles from the school, it was easier for me to become an active part of the school.

Although my living situation was great, I had another issue to address. I needed money to pay for my boarding. It was not a large fee, but it was more than I had. This led me to seek employment. I found part-time employment at a local nursing home, where I served as a Male Attendant, working 25-32 hours each week. I worked there for the duration of my studies at Livingston. That meant that I had to learn how to operate on limited sleep. I often worked the 11 pm to 7 am shift. Sometimes, this shift became challenging. I once had a required Russian History class at 8:00 am. This was the most difficult class that I had because I could not stay awake during class time. I tried to schedule all of my classes from

11:00 am until early evening, giving myself a few hours to sleep, but this Russian class was only offered at 8:00 am.

Occasionally, I got the chance to visit my mother. She told me to call a day or two before I came, so she would have time to cook one of my favorite meals. After talking for a while, I would often go to sleep; because most of the time I had just gotten off work, or I was getting ready to go to work. Whatever the case, I enjoyed spending time with my mother. Those were memorable days that I shall never forget.

As the time passed, I thought more about my high school sweetheart, Mary. We maintained a friendly relationship during our college years, but we discontinued our boyfriend/girlfriend relationship after high school. Therefore, we dated other people during our college days. But nobody I dated made me feel like she did. I knew that she was the person for me. I don't know who she was dating at the time, but during a break when she was home from college, I visited her and told her how I felt, and she expressed the same feelings. We were reconnecting, and it was not long before I asked her to marry me. She said yes. We were married on August 19, 1978. Our honeymoon was in Pensacola, Florida.

During my college studies, I was also the Pastor of the Bethlehem Baptist Church of Boligee, Alabama. I served there from 1975 until 1979. This church's worship services were on Second and Fourth Sundays. After graduating from Livingston University in 1979, I moved to Huntsville, where my wife was employed at the National Aeronautics & Space Administration/Marshall Space Flight Center (NASA/MSFC). This was over 200 miles from the church. My plans were to find employment in Huntsville where I could work during the week, and on the second and fourth weekends, travel to the Boligee area, live with our relatives, perform my Pastoral duties and travel back to Huntsville on Sunday evenings.

I did find employment in retail management in Huntsville, but our travels back home got to be impossible because of the oil embargo in 1979. I could not find enough gasoline to make the trip. At that time, many gas stations were shut down, and others rationed their gasoline. Often after waiting in a long line, I could only get $5.00 worth of gasoline, and sometimes after long waits the attendant would announce that the gasoline was out. This made it impossible to travel to my church. With regrets, I had to resign. I knew that I would eventually have to leave the church because of the distance and my other plans, but thought that I would serve for another year or two.

I worked and lived in Huntsville for two years, before attending the Interdenominational Theological Center - Morehouse School of Religion (ITC/MSR) in Atlanta, Georgia. Initially, I had planned to teach for one year after finishing college, then go to Seminary. Of course, that did not happen. I was employed as the assistant manager of a shoe store, and within six months, I became the manager. I enjoyed the work; the freedom and the pay wasn't bad in comparison to the salary of a first-year school teacher. Therefore, I never applied for a teaching position. Mary had already adapted to the area because she had gone to college (Alabama A & M University) there for four years. She loved living there. But when I moved there, I was only planning to live there for a year. However, I started to like the city.

Things were really coming together for us as a couple. We had good employment. We became members of a friendly church, where I occasionally preached and participated in other church functions. Things were going so well that my plans for theological education started to fade. On the surface, I started to think that I did not need a seminary degree to do ministry. This grew out of the reality that most ministers in the area that our church associated with did not have a seminary background. They had finished high school and some had gone to college. There were only a few African American Baptist pastors that held a Master of Divinity degree from an accredited Seminary at that time in that city. Of course, there might have been a few who had the "mail in" degrees.

After seeing these ministers who were seemingly doing well in their churches, I started to think that I had enough spiritual insight and education to make my mark on the city as a pastor. In fact, in most of the clergy setting, I discovered that my education surpassed the group. As things were coming together for us as a couple and with my fading view of continuing my education, the city started to grow on me. This was the place that I wanted to live.

Mary and I decided to purchase our first house. It was near our membership church (Progressive Union Missionary Baptist Church; Rev. Herbert Cartwright was the Pastor), a few miles from my job and about ten miles from Mary's work. We enjoyed the house and the built-in grill out back. Two of my brothers who were pursuing their education in the area stayed with us occasionally. Nathaniel was attending Alabama A&M University and Fredrick was attending Drake Technical College. I enjoyed them coming over having meals with us. By this time, my brother Raymond had already graduated from Alabama A&M University and was serving in the Army.

Mary's brother, Curtis Biffle, who had worked in Detroit and other places, as well as, served duty in the Navy, enrolled at Alabama A&M University during the same time that we were in the city. Although I knew him, our friendship grew during this time. I grew up with his wife, Ruby. Her father, Rev. Finest Gandy, was my Pastor for several years. He licensed and ordained me. Curtis and I worked in the same mall. He worked in a department store near the shoe store I managed. Therefore, he often stopped by the store before or after work. Sometimes we would have lunch together. He informed me when their store was going to have special sales. We became brothers as we shared with one another. Even today, he is one of the few people that I go fishing with.

Mary reported to work each day, Monday through Friday at 8:00 am. Our store was in a mall, and it was open Monday through Saturday 10:00 am to 9:00 pm; and on Sunday, 1:00 pm to 6:00 pm. That meant that on some days I opened the store and on other days I closed the store. The Assistant Manager and I shared in the responsibility of opening and closing the store. One morning I was scheduled to open the store, I received a word from the Lord. Mary had left for work and I was still in bed anticipating getting up and preparing for work. As I lay there, I started thinking of how well things were going. I thought about getting in touch with a church that was interested in me becoming its pastor, but there was a sudden shift in thought. I started to think how I had promised God and myself that I was going to commit myself fully to the Lord's work. Further, I felt the presence of God urging me to get back on track and go to seminary at the Interdenominational Theological Center (ITC)/Morehouse School of Religion. In my initial planning, I had also considered Virginia Union Theological Seminary. But this encounter revealed to me that I should attend ITC/Morehouse School of Religion.

After I collected myself, I called Mary and told her about my encounter. I'm sure I didn't explain myself well because she asked me more than once, "Are you alright?" I thought I was alright, but actually I was too shaken to go to work. That had rocked my world. I started to think of Mary's great job and promising career, the new house and all of the other things that we would be leaving. I was in the process of considering becoming a pastor of a small church.

When we shared the news that we were moving to Atlanta with the Biffles, they were very supportive of us. They rented our house until we were able to sell it. Mary stayed behind for nearly a year trying to get a federal job transfer to Atlanta and making the arrangements to sell the house. She lived in our house with her brother and his family until she moved to Atlanta.

In the meantime, we needed a place to store our furniture. I thought of the storage house that my mother had back home, which was empty. I called her to tell her that I had resigned my job, and that I had decided to go to Seminary in Atlanta. She asked me if Mary was going as well, I told her no, not at this time. She said that a young couple should not be separated like that. I told her that she was moving later. My mother was disappointed that I was leaving my good job, my new house, and most of all, my wife to go to another school. She asked me a series of questions to determine if I was thinking clearly. I think that she concluded that I was not thinking clearly. She asked me "why" more than once. I told her that God was leading me to go to school there.

Finally, I got around to asking her if we could store our furniture in her storage house. She said yes, she was glad to help us to do what we felt we needed to do. We set the day and time, rented a U-Haul truck and delivered our furniture to my mother's house. My mother observed my every move. She asked several times, "are you alright." I was glad for that awkward day to be over, because it was clear to me that my mother thought that I had lost my mind.

I moved to Atlanta in January of 1981. I went through orientation with the other students who had started that semester. It was not a large group. In the sessions, they reminded us that we had to be creative to make our mid-year enrollment effective, because many of the classes that were offered the second semester were restricted to the students who had already completed their first semester. For example, History II, Old Testament II and New Testament II required that the student take History I, Old Testament I, and New Testament I, first. During the second semester, there were no first level classes offered.

Therefore, I was forced to decide what I was going to major in early so that the electives that I took were not a waste of time. I majored in Christian Education and Church History. My undergraduate degree was Secondary Education, in the field of Social Science. A large part of my Social Science studies was in history. But even some of those classes required introductory classes for the Seminary. However, in most cases I was able to convince the professors that I had the foundation to successfully finish the class. My starting off track was an extra burden to the learning experience; it took more planning and in some cases I took part two before part one. I attended classes both semesters and during the summer and completed my degree in two and a half years.

Mary moved to Atlanta approximately ten (10) months later. During this time, we only saw each other on the weekends. Since her brother and his family were renting our house, Mary usually traveled to Atlanta on Friday evening and would leave early on Monday morning in time to be at work at 8:00 am. The process of selling the house and searching for a job took longer than we expected. After we closed on the house, Mary still had not been able to get a transfer. She stepped out on faith and decided that she was moving on a specified date even if she did not have a job. As soon as she made that decision, she was able to join me in

Atlanta because God blessed her with a transfer to the Internal Revenue Service, and a few weeks later she transferred to the Department of Defense in Marietta, Georgia. We lived in an efficiency apartment on campus until I graduated with a Masters of Divinity Degree in Church History and Christian Education. After graduation, we moved to Smyrna, Georgia, an Atlanta suburb.

When we left Huntsville, I was the Manager of a shoe store, and I was told by the District Manager that if I needed a job while in Atlanta, to just give him a call. I did not take him up on his offer at first because I was able to secure an ideal part-time job at another shoe store while I attended seminary, but the pay was far less than the other store. Nevertheless, I worked there for two years while completing my degree. Knowing that it could take a while to be called to a church as Senior Pastor; I remembered the offer that my District Manager had made two and a half years earlier. I located his number and called him. He said that my call had perfect timing. He did not have a Manager position open in the Atlanta area, but he had an opening in another city. I told him that I was not interested in relocating. Then, he told me that he had an Assistant Manager vacancy in one of his downtown Atlanta stores. I accepted the position.

There were only three of us who worked in that store on a regular basis. Temporary employees were hired to work on holidays. The store was located in the heart of downtown in the Five Points area. Life was busy in that setting. The flashing lights and sirens of police cars, fire trucks and ambulances were seen and heard throughout the day. The park that was located across the street from us, attracted a large number of homeless people. There was always some type of argument, fight or drama in the park.

Women shoe stores are known to be more productive than men.

Men usually buy a black and brown pair of shoes, or even sometimes a burgundy pair of shoes and wear them for years. On the other hand, women usually purchase various types and colors of shoes throughout the year. Although this was a men's store, we had lots of business during the day. We stayed busy most of the time because there was a large concentration of people downtown during the business hours. We sold casual and dress shoes. We also had running and walking footwear, as well as, other footwear accessories. When we were not busy, we were entertained with action in the park.

I rode Atlanta's rapid transit system, MARTA, from North Atlanta to Five Points, often, sometimes six days per week. We were closed on Sundays. Holidays were our big sales days. The store manager was an older white gentleman from Asheville, North Carolina. He was a friendly person, who was knowledgeable of retail management. I invited him to church on several occasions, but he never came. He said that church was not for him. Besides selling shoes, he had a passion for golfing. He played golf every Sunday. On Monday, he had to endure me talking about what happened at Church, and I had to endure him talking about golf. The full-time salesperson was an African American who was in his twenties. He represented the neighborhood and kept the loud music going. He also influenced me to eat oxtails, because oxtails and rice was his favorite meal. I was surprised that they were as good as he said.

We were a close-knit family. For lunch, sometimes one of us would go out to eat and then bring lunch orders back for the others and sometimes one of us would pick up lunch and we all ate together in the store. We talked about personal issues, and argued about sports and politics. Working there was a good experience. My employment in this downtown store lasted for two years and I enjoyed the work. Naturally, I continued to contact vacant churches that were in search of a Pastor. During this time, I interviewed and preached at several churches, as well as, assisted pastors in their work. Although my pastor in my membership church (Chapel Hill Baptist Church on Northside Drive in Atlanta) gave me opportunities to preach, teach and serve, I still desired to be the pastor of a church. That was the reason I had stopped everything to go to seminary.

After about a year working in the store, I started to wonder had I heard God right. Did God really speak to me, and tell me to come to seminary in Atlanta? I had prepared myself to do His work, but no real opportunity had come. The second year after seminary was the hardest. Many of my Baptist classmates had been called to serve churches; but I was still searching and waiting for God to open a door. Occasionally, someone would call and talk about what he was doing in his new position as pastor; and sometimes he would ask what I was doing. I would reply by telling him that I was still working at the shoe store downtown. Furthermore, my mother, siblings, relatives and friends from my hometown called asking "do you have a church yet?" With my own nervousness concerning my future, those other outside forces made my soul searching more intense.

CHAPTER 3

ATHENS HERE WE COME

At this time, I would only consider churches in the Atlanta area because, first, I did not want to relocate, and secondly, I thought Atlanta was the place I was to serve. Since I was not getting any offers in Atlanta, due to my limited search, I started to think of serving wherever God would call me to serve. I started to send inquiries to vacant churches wherever they were located. But my focus was still on Georgia. I received several opportunities to preach at various churches. I preached at Hill First Baptist of Athens, Georgia and the church elected me in the Spring of 1985 to become its Senior Pastor. Of course, this required another move. I was more than ready to leave, but it was difficult to tell my Store Manager that I had gotten a church that required me to relocate. We said our goodbyes, and I was off to Athens.

At this time, Mary and I had two sons; Sherman Tyrone, two and a half years old, and John Nicklaus was one at this time. My family and I relocated together to Athens. My wife went on leave without pay from her Federal job and worked temporary positions until her transfer to USDA/Farmers Home Administration in Athens came through. Once we arrived there, we had the privilege of playing an active role in selecting the church parsonage. We were located in a pleasant house in a well-kept neighborhood (University Heights) east of the University of Georgia campus. In fact, we later discovered that a number of the residents of the subdivision were employed by the University.

I was captivated by the historical architecture of the Hill First Baptist Church structure. The sanctuary had a very high ceiling, stained glass windows, with a seating capacity of six to seven hundred. A large wooden cross was hung near a window behind the pulpit.

I was later informed that the church had suffered from a bat infestation for the last several years. During that first Spring, I received on the job training chasing bats out of the sanctuary before worshippers arrived. Sometimes bats would show up for worship and fly a few laps in the sanctuary. On those Sundays, there was no need for me to announce the benediction for some people, because the bats would give it with their appearance. The early Spring season was the primary time when the problem was at its worst. We had a pest control professional to service the issues and someone installed a special screen to seal out the bats, but none of these measures were effective.

The bat appearance was dramatic enough, but there were other issues involved. Their habitat was in our church's attic, which was not easily accessible for us. The bat feces and urine had a very strong odor, and we could not remove it. Of course, it was difficult to hire anyone to remove it because there was a fear of being bitten by the bats. During the summer months, we had to use some very strong air fresheners to somewhat neutralize the odor. Last, but not least, the bats were known to carry diseases. Because of this problem, I moved my office from the third level of the church to the basement.

Soon after my arrival at the church, I established office hours. I also spent time visiting the sick and shut-in. Then, I became associated with the various religious and social groups in the area. With this exposure, my itinerary became filled with speaking engagements.

This also kept the church busy because the choir, deacons and ushers served at the churches where we were the special guests.

My sons were small during our stay in Athens. When we left, they were seven and eight years old. Due to my wife traveling with her job, I got to spend a lot of time with my sons. I would pick them up from the daycare center and bring them back to the church. They would often spend their evenings next door to my office in the church nursery. I would have different small group meetings, and they required a minimum amount of supervision. When I had speaking engagements at other churches, I would take them with me and have them sit in a place where I could watch them. Many times, church members would be in attendance, and they would take care of them. Of course, this only happened periodically when my wife was out of town.

Approximately one year after my arrival in Athens, I became a part of the Morning Optimist Club. This was a group of men who sought to help the less fortunate. We met once each week at Shoney's. We had weekly breakfast meetings at Shoney's restaurant to fellowship and discuss ways to fulfill our goals. During the football season, we raised funds from a concession stand in the University of Georgia stadium. This means of fundraising was very successful, although the faithful few did most of the work. My wife and sons often joined us as we sold hot dogs, chips, sodas, etc. The experience of being at the stadium on Saturdays, with my family was great. It was wonderful to see our sons running around in the concession area having fun.

We frequently visited the local parks because our sons enjoyed racing with one another and being outside. We threw footballs, baseballs and played basketball. We also spent a lot of time playing games in our backyard. I loved kicking the football to my sons.

However, usually, I would regret it the next day because of a swollen knee. For a brief period of time we had a puppy. As he grew and became larger, he became too aggressive to manage. It got to the point where my sons were afraid to go into the backyard where the dog was kept. I was apprehensive about getting rid of the dog because a member of the church had given it to us, and from time to time would ask how the puppy was doing. However, the situation dictated that the dog had to go!

While in Athens, I gained thirty to fifty pounds in a short period of time! This quick weight gain caused several health issues: high blood pressure, digestive problems, heart pulsating and I just felt bad. I had visited the doctor before, but one day, I felt so bad that I went to the emergency room. After checking in, I was seen by a physician who asked a battery of questions concerning my diet - what and how often did I eat. She asked me about my water intake and exercise. My diet was not good, first of all, I would drink about a pot of coffee per day. I ate at least three meals per day. I ate fried food, greasy food, sweets, sodas and whatever else was presented to me. The doctor concluded that I did not need any medication; all I needed was better self-health management. She told me to cut back on the meats, sweets, coffee and fried foods. She instructed me to drink at least eight glasses of water each day, and walk thirty minutes each morning. She scheduled a follow up visit in three weeks.

I was pleased that the tests did not reveal any major issues; but I felt skeptical about whether her recommendations would correct my problems. Nevertheless, I made a commitment to try her recommendations and started a healthier living routine. I walked in our neighborhood every morning. I started to run back because often I did not leave in time to walk back within the thirty minutes allotted. With walking, running and eating healthy, I was surprised with the energy that I had. I felt good. I did not need the coffee pick me up throughout the day any more. I stopped eating pork and ate very little beef. At the end of the three weeks, both the physician and I were pleased with my results.

With the University of Georgia's first class cushioned track a few miles from our house, I started to run daily. I ran five miles a day, seven days a week. I only missed a few days out of the year. I lost weight and became an advocate of exercising and healthy eating. This became a part of my lifestyle to this day, and it has also influenced my family.

The most memorable occasion during my work in Athens was when my Pastor, Rev. Finest Gandy, my home church, St. Matthew Baptist Church and friends visited our church from Eutaw, Alabama. They traveled to Athens by bus. My mother and grandfather were a part of that group. They came as a part of one of my Pastoral Appreciation Celebrations. They were scheduled to play a leadership role in the 11:00 am worship and a guest church from Atlanta was to lead worship during the 3:00 pm service.

My home church arrived late because the bus driver got lost. It was in the later portion of the service when they arrived. I was preaching when they walked through the doors of the Sanctuary. Just to remind you, we did not have cell phones and other convenient means of communication as we do now during that time. Therefore, we did not know what was causing them to be late. When they entered the place of worship, I knew that things were well. My Pastor knew that it would be a challenge to get there on time for the 11:00 am service, but he set an itinerary that he thought would assure a timely arrival. However, he had not planned that the bus driver would get lost. It was a four-hour drive; but what made it even more difficult was our time was one hour ahead of theirs.

It was a bittersweet moment. They were safe, but their choir did not sing and my Pastor did not preach. However, they were able to witness the last part of that service. Afterwards we fellowshipped, and I took them on a brief tour of the city of Athens and our home while the food was being prepared at the church. We returned and had dinner with the guest Pastor and church, Rev. Larry Jones and the Mt. Zion Second Baptist Church of Atlanta for the 3:00 pm worship. Pastor Jones brought a large group of people. Therefore, the church was filled with members; a bus load from Alabama, more than two busloads from Atlanta, and with other local visitors and friends. I enjoyed the fellowshipping, eating and worshipping.

Probably, more than a few times, I expressed that I had a desire to teach outside the church. The church leaders reminded me that I was the full time Pastor of the church. Other such ventures would make me more unavailable to the membership. I could not argue that truth. But I was already pursuing a doctoral degree at Emory University with aspirations to do some limited teaching in a religious setting. Consequently, I started thinking that I had to make a transition to another setting with a different model of ministry.

I started to work on the Doctor of Ministry degree at Emory University/Candler School of Religion in 1987. As I got closer to finishing this degree, the Liberty Baptist Church in Atlanta caught my attention. I submitted my resume and was given the privilege to meet with the Pulpit Search Committee, lead and preach in one of their worship services. Several months later, the invitation was given and I accepted to become the Senior Pastor. Although Liberty and Hill First were similar in several ways, Liberty was in Atlanta where there were more opportunities.

Things were going well in Athens. The city was just the right size; it was not far from Atlanta; Mary was advancing on her job; the boys had friends, and loved their schools and teachers; and the church where I was serving was embracing our ministry more and more. This was a hard move, but we relocated back to Atlanta to serve the Liberty Baptist Church in July 1991. Again, Mary had to leave her job and move back to Atlanta. After approximately three months on leave without pay, she was blessed to transfer to another agency of the federal government - the General Services Administration (GSA). It did not take my sons long to find new friends and they adjusted well to their new school. We lived in an apartment in College Park, Georgia. One year later we moved to our home in Riverdale, Georgia.

I completed my Doctor of Ministry degree from Emory University in May 1992, one year after accepting the pastorage of Liberty Baptist Church. In fact, during my first year at Liberty it was understood that I was working on my dissertation. Because of the convenient location of the church from the school, my many trips to the library and meetings with my advisor was less stressful than my Athens experiences. After completing my degree, I became more active in launching new ministries at the church; preaching and teaching at other churches; fellowshipping with clergy and denominational groups; participating in community meetings and forming partnerships with other churches in the city. I became overwhelmingly, unconsciously busy because I was finally at the point in ministry where I was called to. Actually, I attended school in Atlanta because I felt called to Atlanta to study and serve as a Senior Pastor. When I went to Athens for six years, I was somewhat confused; because before going there, God had already shown me the place where I was going to serve and I thought that place was in Atlanta. On my first visit to the Hill First Baptist Church in Athens, I was taken to the sanctuary from the basement route. We went up the stairway through the back entrance. This was the exact scene that I had seen in my vision! Therefore, before the church gave me the call, I knew they would. I served the church six years thinking that this was the place that I was going to serve until retirement.

Chapter 4

My Years at Liberty Baptist Church-Atlanta

Six years later, when I went to Liberty Baptist Church in Atlanta, everything started to make sense. I went to Athens to prepare to serve in Atlanta; and the strong clear vision that I had of the stairwell was necessary for me to go to Athens and serve as if that was my lifetime station. After the full circle was made, I was very excited to finally be in the place that I had been shown in the Spirit while I was living In Huntsville, Alabama years earlier.

As stated earlier, while we were living in Huntsville, my thoughts to go to Seminary had started to fade because my wife had a great job as a Contract Specialist, with advancement potential with NASA/Marshall Space Flight Center and I had a good job as the manager of a shoe store. We purchased a nice house and I was considering accepting a church near where I was working. After much prayer and meditation on the issue, one morning in October of 1980, after my wife had gone to work, the Spirit revealed to me that I was to drop everything immediately and go to Seminary at the Interdenominational Theological Center/Morehouse School of Religion (ITC/MSR) because that is where I was to do ministry! I was shocked and when I told my wife, she was shocked. Nevertheless, I was not hesitant to be faithful to that voice that I knew was God's. I had already been accepted at the school some time earlier, but I had postponed my attendance. I called ITC/Morehouse School of Religion in October of 1980 and told the Dean, Dr. Bobby Joe Saucer that I wanted to start school in January of the next year. He told me that it would be best for me to start the fall of the next year. He gave me reasons why starting in the middle of the school year was disadvantageous; all grants and special funding had already been assigned, my classes would be off track and the available apartments were already filled. I told him that I still wanted to come in January. Within a few days he worked things out, and called me to inform me that I was set to come in January and the confirmation was in the mail.

My tenure at Liberty started on July 14, 1991. Dr. Melvin H. Watson retired after serving the church for thirty-two (32) years. He had also served simultaneously as a dean and professor at Morehouse College. Upon his retirement, he became Pastor Emeritus. After several months of my tenure, he requested a meeting with me. In that meeting, he expressed his full support of my ministry. I had asked him to preach on a few occasions; but in that meeting he requested that I would do the preaching to establish myself in the ministry there. He also told me that him and his wife were going to only occasionally be in attendance to give me the space to fulfill my call in that context. Dr. Watson was a wonderful scholar, preacher, teacher and mentor. He recommended to the Morehouse School of Religion Board that I fill a vacant teaching position. His recommendation was accepted and I became Instructor of Baptist History and Baptist Polity. I served the school in that role for twenty (20) years.

For the first few years at Liberty, I intentionally studied the people while they studied me. I visited the shut-ins and listened to the people talk after worship, and whenever we had meetings. They were very friendly and warm. In the previous church, we did not spend a lot of time fellowshipping after morning worship. Those who did not attend Sunday School arrived a few minutes before worship time, 11:00 am. I usually gave the benediction around 12:15 to 12:30 pm. After the benediction, I embraced the members with a handshake or hug. Most often, they quickly went out and got into their cars and departed. There were few exceptions; subsequently, in a few minutes everybody was gone. My family and I were usually among the last to leave. In other words, our leaving the church after worship did not take long.

When we arrived at Liberty, we had to adjust to fellowshipping time. I would do the benediction from the pulpit and go down and station myself in front of the Lord's Supper table, and fellowship with all who came by. Then, I would go upstairs, refresh myself and change clothes. Then my family and I would leave. However, we noticed that after what we considered long fellowshipping time and our preparing to leave, most of the members were still there as we left. Sometimes the fellowship hall would be filled, with people talking, laughing and having a good time.

One Sunday while leaving Mary and I started to laugh, while concluding that we do not have to rush from Liberty because the people really loved being together. There was a youth usher group that occasionally sold punch and popcorn after church. It was amazing to see how the people supported the effort. They ate the popcorn and sipped the punch and water for long periods of time.

After I was getting settled in, we started to accept special invitations to be the special guest at Baptist Associations and Conventions and at various churches for Church Anniversaries, Men's Days, Pastor Appreciations, Youth Days, Revivals, Ordination Services, etc. Of course, when a Pastor received an invitation to preach the entire congregation was invited as well. Many of our members enjoyed the evening services with the fellowship meals and our choir center stage. These "church outings" were motivating to the congregation and myself, while developing fellowship with the churches that we visited. It became common that we invited those pastors and churches to our evening services.

My teaching at the Morehouse School of Religion gave me the opportunity to develop a well-organized ministerial staff at Liberty. Each year, I invited student ministers to join our church, as a part of their practical experience. After completing several sessions with them, I would assign them to lead a particular ministry. In the sessions, we would talk about ministry gifts and interests, and the church's needs during that time. I also placed them on a ministry track, where I would prepare them to preach their first sermon, license them, conduct ordination training, and ordained them. I also assisted them as they sought ministry assignments. In some cases, the student was already a licensed minister. There were even a few who had already been licensed and ordained. However, they all needed a place to complete their Ministry in Context as a requirement of the Master's program at ITC/Morehouse School of Religion.

This ministry was birthed out of my desire to assist female Baptist seminarians who had a difficult time being ordained in their local church because of their gender. They needed the ordination to enter the Armed Services as a Chaplain, or to serve as a Chaplain in a hospital or other institutions. Even in the more liberal Baptist churches that were open to females in ministry, they required the person to be licensed and ordained before being considered for employment. Whatever the situation was, I invited female students to enter our ordination program. In response, many accepted my invitation and became a part of our ministry. We had just as many males attending as well. Many, if not most, of these students were from out of town. Therefore, they were looking for a place to worship anyway.

The first student to complete our ordination program was H. Franklin Harris. He was from the historic Tabernacle Baptist Church of Augusta, Georgia. He served with us the three years that he was in seminary at ITC/Morehouse School of Religion. We finished his ordination process and I ordained him at his home church in Augusta shortly before his graduation. We recommended him to a church in San Antonio, Texas. He accepted the invitation and became the Pastor of that church.

Many of the students who participated in our ordination program became pastors and chaplains in churches and intuitions throughout the United States. On special occasions, we have been blessed to have them as special guest preachers. I have also been invited to their settings of service to preach. Over my twenty-year tenure as Baptist History and Polity Professor at ITC/Morehouse School of Religion, we were blessed by the student seminarians. The other ministers on the staff have also been enriched through this effort.

The other seminary and student project that helped to develop me as a pastor/teacher was serving five years as a Mentor/Professor at United Theological Seminary in Dayton, Ohio from 2003 to 2007. It all started when a member of Liberty, Dr. Wanda Patterson, told me that she had a brother who was a preacher and professor at a seminary, and sometimes he visited with her in his travels. I told her that perhaps he could preach for us sometime when he was in town. We spoke to one another by phone and I asked him when he was going to be in town again? It just so happened that it was on one of our special days and we needed a guest speaker. I invited him, and he accepted. We connected immediately.

It was through our conversation on the Sunday he preached that he made me aware that he was the Dean of the United Theological Seminary Doctor of Ministry Program, and he was seeking to hire a person with a background in Christian Education. He asked would I take the job. I did not know that he had already checked my background. I was shocked and pleased to receive the invitation, but I thought that I did not have the time to perform the duties, which required constant travels and a lot of time with the students. In the next few weeks, I prayed; discussed it with my wife, who had a busy travel schedule; considered my pastoral duties; my teaching at ITC/Morehouse School of Religion; and everything else I was actively participating in. I finally told Dr. McNair that I would try it for one year.

I researched the school and its method and process for the program. I also had to develop a statement of purpose for the particular area that I was leading. Dean McNair's secretary, Janice, was helpful in my preparation for the first session. The first convening weekly meeting with the students and faculty was mid-January of 2003. We met on United's campus, with classes in a large nearby United Methodist Church. There were approximately two hundred (200) students. On the first day, there was a faculty meeting, then a special training for the new faculty. We had an opening worship service during the mid-day. The dean came forth, introduced the faculty, gave information concerning the program, and directions for the week.

Each Professor/Mentor was directly responsible for six students. That first semester, I was assigned three students. That was due to the fact that this was the first time for that area of study; but as time passed, during the other semesters, I had more than my share. The week was intensive. It was packed with teaching, special meetings, and worship. The worship time was important because in various ways it embodied the program of studies, through preaching, lecturing, and dialogue.

Although, we only had one large weekly meeting per semester, we had a group meeting, and met with each student as needed. Of course, there were many conferences with students and with the school. The program required that I be present in/visit the contexts of the students, which was in various places throughout the United States. Most were in church settings. Often when I visited, the students scheduled me to lead a seminar, workshop, or conference. When my schedule would allow, I preached on Sundays. Even though I enjoyed this work and the fellowship with the students, after five years, I felt a need to spend more time at my church and at home. During this five-year period fourteen (14) students received Doctor of Ministry degrees under my leadership.

Another ministry that was of great interest to me was Liberty's Homeless Ministry. After interviewing Ms. Shirley Lewis, a member of the church, I was given a good perspective of the development of that ministry. She said that it was started in September of 1989, by Deacon Oliver Key, who had a passion for the homeless. Initially, the church provided a full breakfast every first Saturday of the month. The ministry grew. In 1991, a full breakfast was being served on the first and third Saturdays of each month. From time to time, haircuts and clothing were also provided. The church membership strongly supported this effort.

The ministry came into existence because the church was in the context of homelessness. In other words, the need was obvious. People often stopped by the church and asked for assistance. More imminent than that, people slept beside and behind our church. Therefore, it was sad to see people living in this state.

During my tenure, we have expanded this outreach to every Saturday. The Atlanta West Pentecostal Church of Lithia Springs, Georgia has partnered with us in this effort. We have a full worship for those who wish to participate; singing, preaching and special prayer and baptism, when needed. For breakfast, we serve coffee, hot chocolate, and a bag breakfast. Occasionally, haircuts and clothing are provided.

As an extension to this outreach, Deacon Charlie Anderson has led a Meals on Wheels project for several years. The frozen food is delivered to the church on Friday, and Deacon Anderson coordinates people to deliver this food to senior citizens and others in need on Saturday morning. Additional ministries have performed special services cleaning up the neighborhood, cutting grass, and painting for seniors.

The consciousness of homelessness led me to seek ways to do something, however little, to address the need. I researched Habitat for Humanity and we partnered with the Redeemer Lutheran Church of downtown Atlanta. We built one house per year for three years. This was difficult because of our share of the cost and our building day was on Saturday. On Saturdays, our service type members would be involved in other outreach ministries. Furthermore, this was the day that we had weddings, funerals and special meetings. Therefore, we started to assist other groups that were sponsoring houses.

The story of the Good Samaritan speaks to the type of ministry that we do in our context. Often there is someone in the ditch needing help; but the very person that we assist may be the person that steals your laptop, or breaks into your car. As a full-time Pastor, I experienced too many cases to recount. But allow me to give just one case in point. Some years ago, we had a young man, who had just turned seventeen (17) years of age, to become a member of our church. During that time, I taught the new membership class. Since he was the only person in the class at that time, he told me about his troubled life. With no father in the house he had been in and out of the juvenile delinquency. He asked that I become his mentor. For a few months after he completed the class, we would talk each Sunday. He made progress as I mentored and encouraged him. One Sunday, it was my birthday and our Church Anniversary, he got my car keys, stole my car and wrecked it a mile away. Thankfully, the young man was not hurt. But, I was very disappointed with his actions.

On another note, while serving Liberty I became very involved in denominational work, especially with the State Convention. I served on the leadership team with the Congress of Christian Education. The Congress provides the teaching leadership for the Convention. Our largest teaching event is the annual Congress in July, which convened on Sunday evening and dismissed on Thursday afternoon. We met at a standard site annually. Members would travel by cars, vans, and buses from various locations across the state of Georgia. There would be classes for all ages and interests. The beautiful grounds and facilities were designed for conferences of this sort. Therefore, we lived in dormitories and had three meals per day. Not only were there sufficient classrooms, there was a large assembly hall for our larger meetings. This was a white operated organization. Members in our organization complained about racism.

In one of the sessions, we had a meeting regarding moving the congress to another location. In that meeting, someone reported that they had done research and determined that there was property for sale in middle Georgia. A few months later, we purchased that property and started to develop it for our purposes. To my disadvantage, I became the President of the Congress the year that we transitioned to our new site. Two buildings were located on the site - an old dormitory that could accommodate no more than twenty people and an old cafeteria that needed many upgrades. However, the grounds were beautiful with a lake and a first-class swimming pool. Since we did not have dormitories to accommodate the delegates, we negotiated with a local hotel for housing. We secured a caterer to provide the food and rented a large tent for our general assemblies and class space. The classes were held under the tent, in the cafeteria, the dormitory and in a nearby church. The Congress was held in mid-July, and afternoon thunderstorms were common in that area. I have my share of memories of over a hundred of us sitting under the tent during a windy thunderstorm, hoping and praying that it would not be blown away. I served four years trying to make our new home work.

Of course, I continued to perform my regular Pastoral duties at Liberty. This position, my teaching in other institutions, and serving in other capacities kept me extremely busy. With the help of my wife, we took mini vacations periodically. She also encouraged me to take a real day off from work each week which was difficult for me to do.

The final project that I want to share with you is our church building project. This was Major! This building project wore me out! For one thing, I never stopped all of the other things that I was involved in. In fact, the project gave me more exposure for ministry opportunities. People became more aware of who we were and the work that we were doing.

We were aware of the need for major renovations to our building.

But it took a number of years for us to conclude to build a new building on our present site. It was a challenge to keep the congregation together because in such situations people had a diversity of perspectives. Then, there was the challenge of generating the necessary funds for the project.

After the congregation decided to demolish our old building and build a completely new building, to our surprise several community and political leaders contacted us. The key spokespersons were concerned that our new building would not represent the historical area that we were in, and most of all, they did not feel good concerning our demolishing of a sacred place of worship. They proposed that we delay the project and offered the possibility of helping us to obtain a grant to renovate our current structure. I could not accept their proposal because we had sought their assistance earlier concerning a grant with no results. In addition, the grant amount was not sufficient enough to make much of an impact on the project.

During the building process, we were able to secure a place of worship approximately one mile away. There were many problems and delays during our building process. Although we tried to follow all the rules of how to plan to avoid change orders, they kept coming! Therefore, we always needed more money. We finally were able to enter our new building on Father's Day 2007. We are now in the mode of maintaining what we have built. But overall, we are pleased to be in a modern facility where we can serve, fellowship, learn and worship.

Things were coming together!

CHAPTER 5

WHEN LIFE MAKES A U TURN

It was not until I was in my mid-thirties that I started to have an annual physical exam. Around the age of thirty-eight (38), after my visit, my primary physician informed me that he had noticed an abnormality in my blood. Therefore, he referred me to a hematologist. Following testing and consultation with that physician, no conclusion was made. My primary physician continued to watch my condition over the years. The numbers stayed approximately the same on each visit.

During the summer of 2008, we had a teenaged relative who was athletic visit with us a few weeks. I had some weights that I occasionally used, but because of his interest in working out, I became more involved in using them. As we were working out one day, my chest made the sound of a big pop. The next day there was a knot on my sternum, therefore I visited my physician. After the examination, he concluded that I had pulled a muscle. Of course, I was told not to do any heavy work for a few weeks, and the situation should correct itself, and it did for a while. However, the knot kept reappearing after lifting the slightest little thing, and then it remained and became painful.

I was hesitant to go back to my primary physician, because on other occasions, he seemed to have felt that maybe I was not giving the situation enough time to heal, before I returned to my regular activities. Therefore, I made a same day appointment with another physician. After the testing, I was sent back to my primary physician. After going through the process of further testing, it was diagnosed that I had the first stage of Multiple Myeloma.

I shall never forget the rainy Tuesday night when my primary physician called and gave me the news. Previously, I have had several tests to determine the problem. I was told that I would be contacted once the results were in. The days passed and I was not contacted, therefore, I called the Doctor's office and asked when would the results be revealed. I was told probably within a few days. After waiting a few days, I made a visit to speak with the doctor, but I was informed that he was attending or involved in a special conference. About this time, I was fully concerned and frustrated with the difficulty of getting the results of my tests. In the meantime, I felt that the results most likely were not good because of the careful way the response was made when I inquired about the test results.

My primary physician finally called me on a Tuesday evening. I had scheduled a Finance Ministry meeting at the church on that evening. Just before the meeting, I got the call, and I was paralyzed with the news. I thought that the result of the tests would be revealed in a sit-down meeting with my doctor in his office, but that was not the case. After spending a few minutes collecting myself, I told the committee that an emergency had come up and I had to go home. I went home and told my wife Mary. That was a long difficult night... In the next few days, we shared the diagnosis with our sons, Tyrone and Nicklaus; my sister and brothers; others relatives and friends. What was most challenging during those first three weeks was trying to get more official information from my primary physician. In fact, when he initially called and gave me the news, I tried to get more information; but he repeatedly told me that this was not his area of specialty. He told me that he was referring me to a doctor who specialized in multiple myeloma, and that doctor would be in touch with me in a few weeks. I repeatedly told him that I needed more information; but his response was the same, "the referred doctor would get in touch with me within a few weeks." Consequently, we googled Multiple Myeloma and read many of the dismal readings defining and describing the fatal consequences of this disease.

Needless to say, my world was turned upside down. During that gloomy time, I was able to find strength and stability in my faith. I started to pray, and the Spirit of Christ revealed to me that God was with me and with us (with my wife and family) as things slowly unfolded. Then, I truly, realized how important it was to have a close fellowship with God. In that moment of revelation, I was empowered to accept my reality and move on. I was able to accept the possibility of early death and I was infused with a new vigor and new vision of sharing my struggles with the congregation that I was serving.

Within approximately three weeks, I heard from the doctor's office that I was referred to. I felt like it was too little, too late. Three weeks is a long time for a person to be put on hold, with questions and concerns. I had to work through the fact that I felt that the system was insensitive and slow moving for a person in a crisis situation.

When I went through another battery of tests, the growth on my sternum was found to be cancerous. I received twenty-eight consecutive days of radiation to treat the cancer. The radiation was successful. I reduced the extensive/intensive schedule of my pastoral duties to enter a chaplaincy program-Clinical Pastoral Education (CPE). That is, I limited preaching at other churches in evening services; doing conferences and workshops/seminars;

attending community, religious and political meetings; and long office hours to have enough time to participate in the CPE experience.

The time of my radiation treatment occurred nearly the same time that I started CPE. This training that lasted for a year and a half strengthened me greatly as I threaded through these major issues of my life. I scheduled my radiation very early in the morning, and reported to my duties by 8:00 am. The nature of the training provided the opportunity for me to share freely how I was working through my illness struggles. Looking back, I am very thankful for my small group critiquing my oral and written presentations. Things could not have been coordinated better.

CHAPTER 6

THE FIRST TRANSPLANT

After studying my condition, my oncologist, Dr. Goldberg, recommended that I consider a stem cell transplant. He referred me for a consultation with Dr. Lawrence Morris at Northside Hospital's Blood and Marrow Transplant Program. Dr. Morris is well-known for his work in this area. Of course, I had heard of transplants; but I had limited knowledge of stem cell transplants. Most of all, I had not related to, or seen it as a part of my world. It was something that I heard on the news, or read in a magazine. Additionally, I thought that it was very risky business.

At the time that I was told that I should consider the transplant, I was feeling well, and it appeared that the medication was effective. However, since I was advised it would not only extend my life, but it would extend my quality of life, I agreed to meet with Dr. Morris. In the meeting, he explained the procedure and the process. Since I did not have any other health issues (high blood pressure, heart conditions, etc.), my risk was very low. I spent a few weeks considering the matter; after which, I advised Drs. Goldberg and Morris that I was ready to go forward with the transplant. I signed a stack of documents and had a battery of initial physical tests. My wife and I also had classes and training exposing us to the program at Northside Hospital.

An important part of the process was to share this information with my family, friends and church membership. They knew that I had Multiple Myeloma, but many could not understand why I would take a risky transplant, when I was doing so well. I think that I was successful in explaining it clearly to most of my immediate family, however, I was less effective with explaining it to my friends and church members. I could tell from their prayers for me, their communications during my recovery and statements they made to me afterwards.

As the time got closer, there were many things to do. I appointed a minister, Rev. Robert Davis, to lead the church in my absence. I had several meetings with him explaining some of the details of his duties and writing and overseeing the writing of the terms of his contract. I also had meetings with the church leaders and membership preparing them for my absence. Rev. Davis proved to be the man for the job. We had many conversations as he merged into his role as leader. Already equipped with the gifts to do ministry, he developed quickly as he carried out his duties.

My wife, Mary was my primary caregiver, which meant that she was going to be with me during the entire process. She was going to drive me to the hospital daily for an extended period of time, prepare and cook my meals and make sure that all of my needs were met. Therefore, because of her leadership role on her job, she had to do extensive briefings to prepare her team for her extended absence.

My transplant was Autologous which means I gave my own stem cells. I was taught how to give injections to myself in order to prepare to harvest my stem cells. Of course, it took placing mind over matter to get through this task. It took several days. Then, it took two days to harvest the cells and they were stored until the day of the transplant. The time for the transplant quickly arrived. I received my chemotherapy treatment for the transplant on November 9th. This date was significant for me in two ways. My mother, Mrs. Addie M. Pelt, was born on November 9th. Secondly, my first grandchild, Andrew Tyler Pelt was born on November 9th. The transplant itself was on November 11th, my brother, Nathaniel Pelt's birthday. These connections made the experience special. My brother represented a sense of roots and family. The birth of my first grandchild reminded me of the future, and it gave me an additional motive to recover, so that I could be a part of his development. Although my mother has been deceased since 1999, I found a sense of strength and communion with her during the early days of the recovery.

I was on medical leave from November 1, 2010 - February 26, 2011. My wife, Mary was with me as my primary caregiver for the entire time.

MY RETURN TO ACTIVE MINISTRY

My medical sick leave ended on February 26, 2011 - day 108 after my transplant. I had longed to get back to the work that I felt called to do; therefore, I returned to the church with a new appreciation, zeal and energy to do all I could to encourage people to fight the good fight of faith. Personally, my worship became more expressive; my preaching and teaching became more piercing and passionate because the reflective time off revealed the joy I got from doing the Lord's work.

On my returning day, I still had a major restriction. I was encouraged not to shake hands and embrace the people because my immune system was still fragile and vulnerable to germs. Therefore, although it was a pleasing and powerful day, it was also awkward. My wife and I arrived at church much later than our usual thirty (30) plus minutes early because we were attempting to avoid having to refrain from interacting with the members, during Sunday

School time and just before people started to arrive for worship. We went directly to my office and remained there until going out to worship at the concluding point of the devotional service. Usually, I attended the Sunday School concluding assembly and proceeded directly to the pulpit prior to the devotional service.

The membership had been told in advance that I should have limited direct contact with them, but some still hugged me or shook my hand. When I entered the pulpit, that was the case. Even then, I felt uncomfortable constantly sanitizing my hands after touching them. Therefore, I started the fist bump in that context. The worship was well attended and the reception of the membership was loving and enthusiastic. I had the privilege of dedicating my grandson, Andrew Tyler Pelt, in that worship. After the worship, there was a reception for our return. But again, I had to discipline myself not to touch people, nevertheless, some still embraced me.

I had been told by my physicians that my merger back into the life of the church should be gradual as I gained more stamina and my immune system got stronger. In those first few weeks, I often became fatigued from teaching and preaching. Even when I did not notice it during the time of ministering, I would be very tired when I got home. I always had to take a nap. As time passed, things returned to some degree of normalcy. I must say, "to some degree," because my experience of battling with cancer drew me closer to God and the spiritual realm. I had a testimony that had to be shared with the church and others. I started dancing in the spirit, speaking in tongues and anointing people with oil. Of course, this caused some conflict in our traditional Baptist Church, as I knew it would. The best response that I could give to those who were concerned was I was doing what the Spirit of Christ was leading me to do. My own struggle moved me to say more about people who were suffering with major diseases.

CHAPTER 7

THE CANCER RETURNS

I imagine one of the most stressful things for a cancer survivor is the fear that the cancer could return. I had my stem cell transplant on November 11, 2010. After I was released from daily, several times per week, and weekly visits, I had follow-up visits every six months. They all went well. But the last test that I had before I started having problems revealed that something was out of balance. After that, I had a few colds, my right elbow started to ache. I had shingles (a very painful condition) and pneumonia. I was evaluated, and it was revealed that a bone leading down to my elbow was deteriorated. I had surgery on that elbow on November 30, 2012. As expected, it was cancerous. It was clear then that the cancer was out of remission and I needed to weigh my options. After having gone through one transplant, it certainly was not something that I wanted to do again. I was blessed to have had very few issues during the recovery from my first transplant; but I saw from other patients what my results could have been. That one was behind me, but I did not know how a second transplant would turn out.

The Autologous (self-donor) is not as complicated as the Allogeneic (outside donor). This time I would be looking at an outside donor, a family member or stranger who would donate his or her stem cell for my treatment. The self-donor was a 90-day process; the outside donor is a 180-day process, if not longer. I was told however that this type of transplant was the most effective. But still the procedure is not a cake walk. My oncologist encouraged me to take the opportunity to live a longer productive life. He also informed me of medications that could extend Multiple Myeloma patient's lives. However, the transplant enabled people not only to live longer, but to live with a much better quality of life. I started the wheels turning for my second transplant in March of 2013.

I had become very busy in the life of the church again, I was preaching revivals, presenting lectures to ministerial groups, participating in Associations, Conventions and School Boards. I had the feeling that this was the worst time to have to pull away and to be absent for months. I did not want to do it. Needless to say, this was larger than what I wanted to do. My transplant physician reminded me that I was in a good state of health to do the procedure. Because I had no other health issues such as diabetes, high blood pressure, or heart problems, my risk of having a successful recovery was higher.

In thinking of life, I confronted the reality that we repair things just for them to come apart again. The repaired lawn mower will not last forever. The repaired automobile will wear out or break down again. Although Jesus raised Lazarus from the dead, he still had to die again. Jairus' twelve (12) year old daughter was healed by Jesus. Possibly she lived a long productive life, but at some point, she died. No, we do not see those people walking or riding around today doing interviews. That means that even those who were healed by Jesus were not eternally healed physically, they got sick and died again.

This revelation helped me to accept my situation, and it helped me to give encouragement to others who were facing similar situations. I had more than one person to ask me if God had performed the miracle of healing on them, could the cancer return, or if the cancer returned, did that mean that there had not been a healing. I believe that we must learn to appreciate miracles whenever they occur, and for whatever period of time that they last.

The Process of Identifying a Donor

The first transplant was an Autologous Stem Cell Transplant, which means that I donated my own stem cells. This was done by first injecting myself twice daily with neupogen, which caused my stem cells to separate from the bone marrow and enter the bloodstream. After several days of this, I went to Northside Hospital's Blood and Marrow Transplant Infusion Facility and was connected to a machine that drew my stem cells. In my case, it required two separate days to harvest the sufficient number of stem cells for the transplant. These stem cells were frozen and stored until my transplant which took place several days later.

However, the Allogeneic Stem Cell Transplant is much different. It involves harvesting stem cells from another person, which is much more complicated than the Autologous, which is self-given. First, they did a national and international search through their registry. I was told in advance that there was a slim chance of identifying a match, because I needed an African American donor. Before then, I was not aware that the closest match realistically had to come from my own race. The reason why the chances were minimal of locating a donor from the registry of donors was that African Americans are reluctant to give blood, platelets, and stem cells.

This fact caused me to reflect on the mindset that I have observed in Black communities that I have been a part of. By saying this, I am not attempting to say that my observation is true for all African Americans; but only for those that I have had the opportunity to interact with. In most cases, this seems to be the case. On many occasions, I have heard, "I just can't stand the sight of blood."

Consequently, I would say that there is a blood phobia in the African American community. During my college years, I remember participating in blood drives on a small college campus. It was difficult to recruit donors. I have noticed this on a number of occasions. We have a health ministry at our church but we have not gotten far with the idea of blood drives. In addition, I think that a part of the landscape of not participating in blood drives, is the fear of shots; of being injected by a needle. Consequently, after evaluating my limited experiences of the mindset of the perspective of many African Americans having negative impressions toward giving blood, I can understand why the national and international registries of stem cell donors is very limited. This revelation fits what I have experienced.

Now back to how my donor was identified. After the computerized approach didn't produce anything for me, we moved to the next step of contacting my siblings: my sister Juanita; my brothers; George, Raymond, Nathaniel and Fredrick. Of course, they were aware of my illness and the previous transplant because I communicated with most of them often. I told them that I needed another stem cell transplant, and they were the prospects for that to be successful. I had lost contact with my older brother at the time; therefore, I was not able to talk to him at this point. Before I could get through the details of what was required to be tested for being a donor, each told me that they were there for me. Subsequently, I confirmed their mailing addresses so that the hospital could mail the testing kits to them. After the kits were mailed, I waited for my sister and brothers to complete the tests and forward their results to a specific address. After a few weeks, the hospital coordinator of this effort, called to inform me that they had not received any of the kits from my sister and brothers. Thus, I called my siblings to see what was the problem. Although they only needed to swab an instrument in their mouth in a specific manner, they were hesitant to do the tests themselves, because they wanted to be sure that the tests were being done properly. Consequently, they asked if there was a specific medical facility that needed to do the tests. In the conversations, each decided to do the tests themselves, or have their Doctor's office or local hospital administer the test. After a few weeks, the tests were mailed and the results were shared. My three brothers were half matches - 5/10; which made them acceptable donors; but my sister, Juanita was a perfect match, 10/10! After the test results were in, I called each person to give them the good news. Shortly afterward, my older brother, George, who we were unable to contact initially, called to let me know that he was available to do the testing. I told him that I was thankful of his offer, but Juanita had already agreed to be my donor because she was a perfect match.

On May 22, 2013, Juanita took a bus from Tuscaloosa, Alabama and arrived in Atlanta that evening before 7 pm. Mary and I picked her up after Bible Study and traveled home. We spent a brief part of the evening talking, but we didn't talk long because we both had a cough. We went to bed early anticipating the day ahead of testing at Northside Hospital. I had already done my testing in preparation for the transplant. The next morning, Thursday, May 23rd, Juanita, Mary, and I got up early and drove to Northside Hospital's Blood and Marrow Transplant (BMT) Infusion Facility where Juanita received a thorough physical examination. After the tests were completed, Juanita was invited to the conference room. I accompanied her, but the convener of the meeting told me that they only needed to meet with my sister. Therefore, I returned to the lobby.

Once the meeting with Juanita was completed, I was called into the same conference room. As I was leaving the lobby, going to the conference room, she was entering the lobby. I could tell that the news was not good. When I met with the medical coordinator, she first apologized for not allowing me to be a part of the conference with my sister. She explained the hospital's policy concerning the patient's privacy rights. I told her that I was aware of the policy because I was trained in a local hospital as a chaplain. Then, she told me what she could with those restraints. They recommended that we not consider my sister as my donor because she had her own health challenges. Needless to say, our ride back home was a difficult one. She thought that I had been given more information about her condition than I had. On the other hand, I thought that they had given her the specific condition that they found. She told me that she regretted that she could not be my donor. Most importantly, I was concerned for her well-being. I felt so badly that my sister had just discovered that she had a major health condition.

The next morning, which was Friday, my wife Mary, her Aunt Ozinnia, Juanita and I traveled to Eutaw, Alabama to our family reunion. Juanita lived just eight (8) miles away in the house where we grew up in Clinton, Alabama. Since the passing of our Mother in December of 1999, my siblings and I along with our children & grandchildren, have had a Family Reunion each year in May during Memorial Day weekend. In the beginning we went back home every year, but now we alternate hosting the reunion in the cities where we live.

Back to May 23rd - Nevertheless, before we left our home in Atlanta, Juanita broke down and hugged my neck crying, asking me if I had been told that she had some kind of disease, or cancer? I told her that they only told me that she could not be my donor because she had her own health challenges. We embraced and cried briefly. I went outside and asked Mary and Ozinnia, who were moving and arranging the cars, to please come in. We were going in one of our three cars and parking Ozinnia's car alongside one of our cars in the garage. When Mary and Ozinnia came into the house, they could see how shaken Juanita and I were. We had prayer and gave words of encouragement to one another. Once we had composed ourselves somewhat, we started on our two hundred fifty (250) mile drive to the family reunion. We did not say much at first, but as we traveled the heavy mood slowly evaporated allowing us the chance to talk and enjoy the trip.

All five of my siblings were in attendance at the reunion, and many of our children and grandchildren were present as well. Like what we do at many reunions; we fried fish Friday night; looked at slideshows and photo books, provided by Mary, of previous reunions; made introductory statements; and distributed the family reunion T-shirts. On Saturday (my 58th birthday), we had a cookout with barbeque chicken, hot dogs, beef burgers and all the trimmings.

During those two days, I did not know how to respond to the questions of how things had gone with the testing. Many were aware that Juanita had gone to Atlanta to prepare to donate her stem cells to me within the next several days. In some cases, I was able to respond that things didn't work out because of health issues. It was commonly known that Juanita had some health problems; because we shared some of those known problems with the stem cell team before they had her to come and be tested. However, they felt that her issues possibly would not interfere with the transplant. They could not know for sure until she was examined. Thus, my general reply to those who inquired on the outcome of my sister's physical did not send a real negative impression; because I wanted her to tell the details of her own situation. Being a pastor, my family and I returned to Atlanta Saturday night so that we could be at Liberty for Sunday morning worship.

Within the next few weeks, we spent our days attempting to discern where we would go from there. Naturally, many of us had to adjust our schedules; but we did not know how to fill in the blanks. We had already secured our Assistant Pastor to serve in my absence, who was serving as an interim Pastor in another setting. Rev. Kewon Foster ended his tenure prematurely at the church that he was serving to serve in my stead. My wife Mary, who was going to be my caregiver, already had locked in on her medical leave of absence from her workplace; my brothers who were next in line to be my donor wanted to know the timeline so that they could submit information to their job to be off when needed; all those involved wanted to know what the next move was and when we anticipated the transplant happening. The answer to these questions seemed slow in coming.

After approximately three weeks, I spoke to my doctor. He told me that we had security in my three brothers who were half matches. That meant that either could be used in a successful transplant; but they were in their 50's. He stated that possibly one of my two sons could be a match and they are much younger. Consequently, he recommended that they be tested to see if at least one would be a half match. Both of my sons were half matches. I asked them to decide who would be the donor. The next day, my younger son, Nicklaus called and said that he would be the donor. He had the required physical and was cleared to prepare for the surgery of removing his stem cells.

THE ROUTINE AFTER THE TRANSPLANT

The week before the transplant, I received high doses of chemotherapy and radiation. After the transplant, I received two additional days of chemotherapy. On the day of the transplant, I checked into Northside Hospital's Blood and Marrow Transplant Unit at 7:30 am, as an outpatient and the medical team prepared me for the transplant. Simultaneously my son, Nicklaus was having his stem cells surgically removed in a clinic nearby. At 11:58 am the infusion process started and at 1:38 pm it was completed. I have a vague memory of the transplant. I had lunch at 2:10 pm. I received one unit of blood at 4:50 pm, and was dismissed at 7:20 pm.

Starting the next day after the transplant, I had to visit Northside Hospital's Blood and Marrow Transplant (BMT) Infusion Facility for seven consecutive days. I had two caregivers during that period of time, Mary, my wife, was my full-time caregiver, and my son, Tyrone was my secondary caregiver. Mary brought me to the BMT Infusion Facility most of the time because she was on a medical leave of absence, and Tyrone brought me a few days when he could. Our son, Nicklaus and my daughters-in-law, Cherline & Chailoea also played their role in caregiving; but Mary brought me to the BMT Infusion Facility most of the time, and spent the day with me.

Each morning, we would get up at 5:15 am and be ready to leave home by 6:40 am so that we could arrived at the BMT Infusion Facility by 7:30 am for our 7:45 am appointment (initially the appointment was at 7:30 am, but it was later changed to 7:45 am). After parking in the garage on the second level most of the time, we caught the elevator and rode it to the 8th floor; got off, and caught the second elevator to the 10th floor; then, entered the lobby of the BMT Infusion Facility. Most times the lobby would be filled with patients with masks on their faces, and with caregivers, waiting for names to be called to go to the next steps. When my name was called, I would be weighed, vital signs checked and blood would be given. Then, I would go to the site where I would remain for several hours while being treated. Most times, I would receive fluids, and other treatments according to what the blood tests revealed that I needed. Occasionally, I received blood and/or platelets. There was a special nurse assigned to my care, but on the weekend, I had different nurses. My caregiver (my wife Mary) also stayed with me during the time of my treatment. There was a chair for the caregiver in every treatment area. There were twenty-three in the complex and they stayed filled with patients and caregivers.

Usually after the treatment, we would make the necessary stops at the pharmacy, grocery story or our bank. Of course, I had to remain in the car while Mary took care of whatever needed to be done at these stops. We went home and had lunch; took a brief nap; read and wrote; looked at a few selected TV programs and went to bed early so that we could be refreshed for the next day. During our time at the BMT Infusion Facility, we talked, read, wrote, checked and responded to emails and sent and received text messages. It was not a setting for speaking on the phone. I also would walk several laps in the BMT Infusion Facility daily, while rolling the pole that held my intravenous treatment. In the early days of the transplant, my white blood count stayed on zero for five days. That meant that my body had no ability to fight off germs. I had to be very careful not to touch anything that could have any germs. I washed or sanitized my hands constantly.

The routine of the recovery became not so routine when the various side effects occurred. I was taking a medication that caused my kidneys some problems, but I needed the treatment to help keep me from catching pneumonia or other respiratory problems. Then, on September 25, 2013, I was getting ready to go to the BMT Infusion Facility and Mary was anticipating her retirement celebration. On that morning Mary noticed that there was something strange about my left shoulder. When I felt it, there was a knot near the size of a golf ball.

ISOLATION AND THE REASONS BEHIND IT

The treatment of Multiple Myeloma and similar diseases that require stem cell transplants demands a long recovery period, where the patient must be in various levels of isolation, depending on their progress and the general length of time of the treatment. With the Autologous Stem Cell Transplant, it usually takes the patient 100 plus days to return to work, school, or a normal schedule. In my first transplant, I returned on my 108th day. The Autologous transplant is a self-donor transplant; where the stem cells are harvested from the individual, frozen, and given back to that person after chemotherapy and other treatments.

On the other hand, the Allogeneic transplant is when another person is the donor. This type of transplant requires more time to initiate and to recover from. In my case, it took approximately four months to locate a donor. The recovery time was estimated to be 180 days with an evaluation of 100 days post-transplant. In addition, other tests and evaluations are made to determine when the patient is ready to re-enter the regular routine of life.

During my first transplant, I felt well enough and strong enough to return to worship after the first month; but I could not because I was aware of the vulnerability of my immune system. With the second transplant, I felt good enough to attend within the first month, but the same was the case. Therefore, one of the frustrations of the recovery is that the patient might feel well enough to travel, go to restaurants, shop in the mall, socialize in group settings, return to work; but that is not advisable because the slightest germ could compromise the person's immune system and cause a major health challenge.

The education that the health team provides before and during the transplant is very important to limiting the possibility of contracting germs. Initially, we were taught lessons on the function of the immune system, and the role that it plays in fighting off germs. Other material and handouts were presented. During the treatments, Nurses, Physician Assistants and Physicians reminded us of the various precautionary measures to utilize to protect ourselves from germs.

The patient is Neutropenic immediately after the transplant. This is when the immune system is at its weakest point, and it takes approximately two weeks for it to start to reactivate. Unless there are some other complications that caused the patient to be in the hospital, the patient is driven to the BMT Infusion Facility at the hospital daily by their caregiver. Upon arriving to and departing from the BMT Infusion Facility, the Neutropenic patient is advised to wear their mask when they get out of the car, not to touch the outside handle of the car door, or the railings in the building, or the elevator button, or any item that could be contaminated with germs. We are also encouraged to sanitize, or wash our hands often.

During this period, a special food list is provided. If eaten raw, fruits and vegetables must be prepared with special care, to make sure that all of the bacteria and fungi are removed. I did not take a chance eating fresh apples, oranges, grapes, strawberries, plums or pears during this time. I ate bananas and watermelons; which surfaces could be easily cleaned. The cooked food had to be prepared and cooked carefully. There is no eating at restaurants or fast foods chains, because public eateries are known to have germs that transplant patients cannot tolerate. Therefore, for 100 days, Mary prepared my meals at home.

When it comes to being in face to face contact, I did come in contact with people while going to, or returning from my treatment. Of course, I had my mask on. Once we entered the BMT Infusion Facility, I could remove my mask. I was told that there is a special air circulation in the BMT Infusion Facility designed especially for this type of treatment.

The chemotherapy, radiation, and strong medication cause many different side effects to include: nausea, vomiting, loss of appetite, constipation, diarrhea, bleeding, headache, stomach ache, urinary problems and a host of other things. I had limited nausea and I vomited once after taking chemotherapy treatment in preparation for my transplant. One major side effect for a week to ten days was with my urination. I stayed in the restroom; and what was so frustrating was sometimes I did not make it to the restroom. On many occasions in route to and from my treatments I had to utilize a portable urinal!

THE SUPPORT SYSTEM

The support of family, friends and others plays an important role in the recovery of patients. In my case, my wife, Mary was my primary caregiver. She took a medical leave from work from July 29 through September 27, for 61 days to make sure that all my unique needs were met. She drove me 27 of the 29 consecutive days that I had to go to the BMT Infusion Facility. In addition, she drove me most other days that I went. I remind you that during this time, I could not drive (for six months), go inside grocery stores, restaurants, movies or any places where there was a crowd (with the exception of the BMT Infusion Facility), because my body could not control even everyday germs. In the first month, I had to be very careful touching surfaces and being in an environment that could challenge my health. Therefore, I had to wash or sanitize my hands constantly; and I used my mask often; my food had to be prepared with special care. There was a time in the treatment when I was encouraged not to touch the mail, the mail box, the door knob, the car handle, the elevator button, shake hands, touch money or anything else that was not sanitized.

Consequently, Mary prepared my meals three times a day; she washed my clothes; screened my calls; managed my medication; sanitized my environment; completed medical insurance and other documents; took out the trash; opened my car door and house door; touched the button for the elevator; got the mail; read my mail to me; handled the money; proofed my writings and did all the other things that were needed to be done to ensure that things ran smoothly. At the same time, although, she was officially on leave from her job, occasionally she still had conference calls. She did all the work, driving me to the clinic, cooking, cleaning, washing, sanitizing and taking care of business, while I spent my day being treated, reading and writing on the two works that I wanted to complete during my medical leave. There were times when I had to encourage her to take a break and get some rest. She was the greatest during the first transplant, as well as this transplant.

Our oldest son, Tyrone was also my caregiver for this second transplant, although, he was very busy on his job, studying for a special engineering certification and having a new house built, not to mention the fact that he and his wife Cherline have a very energetic two and a half year old son, Andrew. He picked up items for us from the store and brought us packages from members of the church. His wife, Cherline, came over and assisted us in every way she could.

Our son Nicklaus, was my donor. What more can a person do for you? He and his wife Chailoea made sure that we had what we needed. Like with Tyrone and Cherline, they were very busy with their jobs, this was Chailoea's first year as an elementary teacher; but they systematically found the time to check on us.

My siblings and I communicated often during my recovery. My oldest brother, George as well as my nephew Chris called often to see how I was doing and to talk about the autobiography that I was writing.

Church members provided great support through their prayers, cards and other expressions of love. It was uplifting to be able to stay in contact with the membership during this 2nd transplant via phone & conference calls, email and text messages.

Communications and acts of kindness from friends and colleagues also assisted in my recovery. For example, Dr. Marsha Harris sent a CD of some of her son's sermons. Her son, Rev. H. Franklin Harris was my first Associate Minister and ITC/Morehouse School of Religion mentee. Pastors of congregations have me on their prayer list, where they prayed for me daily, or on Sunday during their special altar call prayer.

With all the expressed love that is in the air, in the environment, the door of possibility is open for physical healing.

STAYING IN TOUCH THROUGH TECHNOLOGY

One of the most challenging things concerning the transplant is that it takes you out of circulation. For me, I longed to be at church at least during Sunday worship. Due to the fact that it is not feasible, I thought of the Apostle Paul who was often in prison, or could not visit the congregation that he wanted to or needed to because of other circumstances. He used what was available to him at the time. There were times when he sent one of his associates to express his concerns and resolve conflicts. There were other times when he sent letters. Most of all, his isolation did not stop his communication with the outside world where he was still spreading the message of Christ.

I thought, if Paul could turn the world right side up, spending much of his time in prison, then I can do something to communicate with the church and others about God's miraculous works in the world today. This led me to consider the various ways that I could keep the communication line open with family, friends, other pastors, and with the church that I serve. This was my concern because I did not do well with communicating with those who were concerned about me. During my first transplant, my wife answered the phone calls, and informed the people concerning my recovery state. I felt disconnected. But when I consider Paul's approach of sending a signal of hope where you are, I am encouraged to do the same. My sons sometimes bring items from members who send us food (most of which I cannot eat), cards and other gifts. The membership sends messages by them, and we respond by sending messages back through them.

During this transplant, however, my basic ways of staying in touch with the outside world are by phone, texting and email. When members, family and friends called, I answered the call or returned it as soon as possible. I had many conference calls with the Assistant Pastor. I also had conference calls with ministry leaders, and with ministries of the church. During my medical leave, the Ministerial Staff created a prayer hotline. We called in on each Tuesday at 7:00 am and had prayer.

During the month of September, we had two members to pass that I was very close to. I felt that I needed to be in attendance; however, I could not be; so, I used the next best thing available, my pen. I carefully crafted a statement for Mrs. Lillie Jackson. My wife read it to those who were in attendance. We did the same for Mother Carnell Harden's homegoing service. Family members were appreciative that we would share in their time of bereavement even though I had my own health limitations.

Each year the church sponsors Pastor Appreciation on the third Sunday in September. Of course, this year, I was on medical leave. The celebration went on as usual. We had Rev. Stanley Kimble, the Pastor of the New Smyrna Baptist Church of Fort Valley, Georgia as our guest speaker. Mary and I had planned to Skype into the worship from our home. However, because of some medical complications, I had to resume daily appointments at the BMT Infusion Facility. Therefore, we were at Northside Hospital on Pastor Appreciation Day (9/15/2013).

Nevertheless, we decided to Skype from the BMT Infusion Facility because I was only receiving fluids, which did not require much medical attention. We dressed in our black and gold, as if we were attending a formal affair. When we arrived, we got more attention than we had anticipated. One patient jokingly asked, "why would you come into a place like this, with very sick people, looking like a mortician?" I had on a black suit and a black bow tie.

We told the nurse about the service and she assisted us by getting a private room where we could interact in the worship. We Skyped into the service and gave greetings. Then the worship continued. Within a few minutes, we lost internet service. We moved back into a general area where the reception was usually better; but it wasn't on that day. We had recently purchased an internet hot spot, which allowed us to use our own internet service. We were communicating with our son Tyrone, who was at the church. After approximately fifteen minutes, we were reconnected. But we were in a semi private location where we had to use headphones, so that we did not disturb the other patients. With the exception of the fifteen minutes we lost connection, we were a part of the worship celebration. Before the benediction, we made a brief statement thanking the people for their many expressions of love. Especially on that evening, and a few days following, we received many phone calls from parishioners who were glad to see us. Although we had several communications with Liberty members, the Skype experience surpassed everything!

WHERE DO WE GO FROM HERE

These are the last words typed by Dr. J. Sherman Pelt on October 6, 2013

EPILOGUE

Dr. Pelt completed the 1st draft – I don't know what he planned to include in this chapter nor do I know how he planned to go back and fill in the gaps... On October 19, 2013, a few days before his transition, when he could no longer write, he asked us (his family) to finish this work. We promised him that we would. I remembered our promise, but I could not even attempt it for a period of time. I prayed for God's help to complete this most difficult task. He answered my prayers and gave me the strength this year of 2020, the year we will commemorate the 7th year since his transition, to complete this extremely challenging assignment. The support and contributions to the publication of this writing by our children has been immeasurable. Praise God from whom all blessings flow!

- Mary O. Pelt

Life Milestones

Written by Mary O. Pelt

After receiving the strength to read through, with tears in my eyes, what my beloved Sherman had completed, I prayed to God for direction on how to include additional information while leaving what he had written intact. God's answer to my prayer was revealed to me at 4:28 am on May 7, 2019. That answer was to include his life milestones. I immediately got up and wrote down some notes, knowing from my own experience and Sherman's experiences I observed over the years, that those revelations may not be there at my regular getting up time. Subsequently, while reviewing the documents from his laptop I was able to locate writings he prepared at significant times in his life. Therefore, his own words are being quoted where indicated in bold print. Praise God exactly one year later on May 7, 2020 I completed the 1st rough draft of the entire book, except for the pictures!

Before moving to the milestone, I would be remiss if I did not express what an honor and blessing it is to have been chosen to share 41 years (35 years as husband and wife) with my best friend, the Rev. Dr. J. Sherman Pelt. He enjoyed life, he was positive, friendly, and outgoing with a great sense of humor. God gave us The Love of a Lifetime. We shared so much - God blessed us tremendously. I am thankful to God for joining us together. I couldn't have found a better husband than the one God chose for me. Over the years, as we labored together in service to God's people, many challenges were encountered along the way. However, as a result, we grew stronger in our faith and closer as husband and wife. It was a delight to share this amazing Christian journey together as God moved us from place to place in accordance with His will.

He was a person who knew, without a doubt, his purpose. He dedicated this entire adult life to ministry. He often said he would rather wear out than rust out when it came to serving the Lord. After serving 4 years as Pastor of Bethlehem Baptist Church (Boligee, Alabama) while attending college full-time, he served as full-time Pastor of Hill First Baptist Church (Athens, Georgia) for 6 years and Liberty Baptist Church (Atlanta, Georgia) for 22 years. A person committed to doing those things that were right and pleasing to God is who he was. We know that he was filled with the Spirit of God because we saw the evidence in his daily life – love, joy, peace, longsuffering, gentleness, goodness, faith, meekness, and temperance (Galatians 5:22-23 KJV).

A person of prayer and of faith with a double dose of the Holy Ghost, this extraordinary gift from God possessed a humble spirit, outstanding dedication, unusual perseverance and remarkable commitment to his calling in life. He preached powerful, piercing and passionate sermons. He loved God and God's people. He was an exceptional Pastor, Preacher, Teacher, Scholar, Leader, Mentor, Friend, Counselor, Confidant, Motivator, and Encourager who gave freely and wholeheartedly of himself; his time, his talent, and his treasure. He was generous, he was a giver, he received great joy from giving; he gave sacrificially. His rich contributions are far reaching and we are better because of his presence in our lives. He is an example of the incredible difference one person can make in this world. During his earthly journey, he touched and poured into countless lives. He made this world a brighter and better place. His works are alive in the many hearts and lives, all across this nation, that he touched and enriched during his life and ministry. He was an inspiration to us all. Many were richly blessed for the special way God's love was expressed through him.

The best father and grandfather, he earned the title "Father of the Year" for the love, devotion, care, and support expressed continuously. We shall forever treasure the precious memories, the joy and laughter we shared. The quality time that we spent together as a family will be cherished always. He will be forever with us in our hearts. Even though our pain and sorrow is still great, God is our strength. He continues to speak to us through His Holy Word: "Fear not, for I am with you; Be not dismayed, for I am your God. I will strengthen you, Yes, I will help you, I will uphold you with My righteous right hand." Isaiah 41:10 NKJV

Our loss is heaven's gain. He was on fire for the Lord down here and we know he is running, jumping, and shouting up there! No more pain and suffering; he has spiritual healing and eternal life! Oh, yes, we miss him and our lives will never be the same, but we are so thankful for all that we shared; God gave us so much by letting J. Sherman Pelt be a part of our lives!

May 25, 1955

John Sherman Pelt was the 3rd child of six siblings born to Mr. John Sherman & Mrs. Addie Montgomery Pelt in Forkland, Alabama. His siblings are: George (now deceased), Juanita (now deceased), Raymond, Nathaniel & Fredrick. He also had an older sister, Evonne Pelt, (now deceased).

"During my early years, my mother was a school teacher. My father was a factory worker and cotton farmer." **(1987 Doctoral Application to Emory University)**

August 1965 (Age 10)

Accepted Christ as his personal Savior on a Tuesday night during revival at St. Matthew Baptist Church; Eutaw, Alabama; Rev. Hall, Pastor.

"At age 10, my mother had me sit on the "mourner's bench" during our annual revival. On Tuesday night during the revival, I gave the Pastor my hand and God my heart. I was not as emotional as some of the rest who confessed Jesus that week (there were 15 of us); but I had a moving spiritual encounter. During the first few months after that, I didn't want to harm a fly; and there were many flies in my context. The revival was the second week in August and the baptism was the second Sunday in September. We were baptized in a large cow pond. Hundreds of people were in attendance. There was great singing, praying and preaching. After the baptism service, we returned to the church for worship. I never will forget that day. However, the next week we received the shocking news that the Reverend Hall had died of a heart attack. For the next weeks and months, I replayed experiences and messages of Reverend Hall in my mind. Now 43 years later, I still clearly remember what he looked like." (2008 Clinical Pastoral Education (CPE) Application)

1965-1966

Repeated the 4th grade. In his adult years as a pastor, this is something he spoke of often relative to how far God had brought him!

"With the changing of the times and our growing up, we stopped farming on a large scale... With the decline of farming, we were able to go to school every day. I got involved in the marching band. I also became a better student and made better grades. I decided that I wanted to attend college." (2008 Clinical Pastoral Education (CPE) Application)

October 1968 (Age 13)

His father, Mr. John Sherman Pelt, Jr. passed.

"When my father died three years later, I went through a crisis. First of all, my Father never did confess belief in Jesus, even though he was sick for 8 years. Secondly, I was very attached to him in several ways. I was named for him; I shaved him every day and cut his hair when it was needed. He told me his many stories. I regretted that he never confessed that Jesus was the Savior of the world." (2008 Clinical Pastoral Education (CPE) Application)

1968

After the passing of his father and maternal grandmother, within months of each other, his mother and siblings moved to Clinton, Alabama to live with his maternal grandfather, Mr. George Montgomery (Gramps), who greatly influenced his life in a positive way.

"My grandfather, who was a farmer, took on the role of father. He taught my four brothers, one sister and I the

dignity of work. During planting and harvesting seasons, we were unable to attend school every day. Often, we only attended school three days out of a week." (1987 Doctoral Application to Emory University)

May 1973 (Age 17)

Accepted the Call to preach the Gospel.

"The church played a vital role in our lives. We were required to attend Sunday School and Morning Worship each Sunday. My grandfather was a deacon and my mother was active in many roles in the church. I confessed belief in Jesus, the Christ at the age of ten. The Christian faith engulfed me more than I had any idea. By the age of sixteen I was a Sunday School teacher." (1987 Doctoral Application to Emory University)

"When I became a teenager, I had dreams and thoughts of being a preacher. While in my junior year of high school, this became so intense that I couldn't eat or sleep. I told my mother and my pastor about my experiences. My pastor spent a lot of time with me helping me to sort out my thoughts and giving me direction. I preached my first sermon on Father's Day in 1973." (2008 Clinical Pastoral Education (CPE) Application)

June 17, 1973 (Father's Day)

Preached his initial sermon. "The Prodigal Son" Text: Luke 15:11-32 at St. Matthew Baptist Church; Eutaw, Alabama; Rev. Finest Gandy,

Pastor.

The following Scripture is one he quoted each year on the anniversary of his initial sermon:

In the year that King Uzziah died I saw also the LORD sitting upon a throne, high and lifted up, and His train filled the temple. Also I heard the voice of the Lord, saying, Whom shall I send, and who will go for Us? Then said I, Here am I; send me. Isaiah 6:1 & 8 KJV

"Due to the popularity of my pastor, my preaching schedule became very busy overnight. I preached Youth Days and Youth Revivals; and other special days and anniversaries at the various churches in the area. My name was constantly on the radio." **(2008 Clinical Pastoral Education (CPE) Application)**

August 12, 1973

Licensed to preach by the St. Matthew Baptist Church; Eutaw, Alabama; Rev. Finest Gandy, Pastor.

May 31, 1974

Graduated from Paramount High School; Boligee, Alabama. He was the Class President and a member of the Marching Band prior to his senior year. He played the trombone. I was also in the Class of 1974.

August 1974

Entered Selma University; Selma, Alabama

"I was eager to go to Selma to learn more about preaching and the church. This Bible College was highly recommended by pastors in the area." **(2008 Clinical Pastoral Education (CPE) Application)**

August 8, 1975

Ordained to the work of The Gospel Ministry by the St. Matthew Baptist Church; Eutaw, Alabama; Rev. Finest Gandy, Pastor.

May 1976

Graduated from Selma University; Selma, Alabama with an Associate in Arts (AA) Degree. While a student there he was a member of the Concert Band, playing the trombone. He also served as President of the Ministerial Alliance.

Transferred to Livingston University (now The University of West Alabama); Livingston, Alabama.

May 1975—August 1979

1st **Pastorage - Served at Bethlehem Baptist Church; Boligee, Alabama while attending college full-time.**

Actively participated in the Mt. Olive Baptist Association as a member and officer.

Active in the Youth Department of the Alabama State Convention.

"I was given many opportunities to preach, especially in special youth programs. After approximately one year of preaching, church after church wanted to elect me as their pastor. However, my pastor advised me that I was still too young and immature to take on such a responsibility. Conversely, a few months later he recommended me to Bethlehem Baptist Church in Boligee, Alabama. I became pastor and served there for four years. Bethlehem Baptist Church was a small congregation. It was comprised of approximately sixty members. Worship service was held on the second and fourth Sundays of each month. I served this church during my college years." **(1987 Doctoral Application to Emory University)**

August 19, 1978

United in holy matrimony with his high school sweetheart, Miss Mary Outland at Mt. Olive Baptist Church; Boligee, Alabama – Officiated by Dr. Ace D. Outland, Jr. (Mary's uncle).

June 2, 1979

Graduated from Livingston University (now The University of West Alabama); Livingston, Alabama with a Bachelor's Degree in Secondary Education and Social Science.

A brick on the Walk of Honor has been donated by his family.

Received certification as a Secondary School Teacher.

> ### March 1979 – December 1980

We lived in Huntsville, Alabama where I was employed with NASA/ Marshall Space Flight Center on Redstone Arsenal.

Resigned as Pastor of Bethlehem Baptist Church; Boligee, Alabama

Served as Associate Pastor of Progressive Union Baptist Church in Huntsville, Alabama; Rev. Herbert Cartwright, Pastor.

Worked as Asst. Manager & Manager of Hardy Shoe Store in Huntsville, Alabama.

> ### January 1981 – May 1983

Matriculated at Morehouse School of Religion at the Interdenominational Theological Center in Atlanta, Georgia.

While attending seminary he worked as a Student Field Counselor with the Fulton & Dekalb County Juvenile Delinquency Correction Centers; a Student Counselor with the Georgia Mental Health Institute; and a Student Researcher at the Southern Legislative Research Council.

He was a member of and served as Associate Minister at Chapel Hill Baptist Church on Northside Drive in Atlanta, Georgia.

Served as Youth Minister at Central Baptist Church in Ellerslie, Georgia (Service concluded in 1984).

"In January of 1981, I entered ITC. I enjoyed the years that I

spent at ITC. Nevertheless, this was a challenging time for my marriage. My wife had a great job at NASA in Huntsville, Alabama; and she was hesitant in giving it up. But God got us through those difficult days.

When I was called to pastor The Hill First Baptist Church in Athens, Georgia; Mary's job was an issue and the same was true when we returned to Atlanta six years later. Each time she regretted leaving a good job with slim prospects of finding one of equal status. But God always came through for us." (2008 Clinical Pastoral Education (CPE) Application)

1982

Son, Sherman Tyrone Pelt was born.

May 14, 1983

Graduated from Morehouse School of Religion at the Interdenominational Theological Center; Atlanta, Georgia with a Masters of Divinity (MDiv) Degree in Church History & Christian Education.

Continued serving as Associate Minister at Chapel Hill Baptist Church; Atlanta, Georgia while searching for a full-time pastoral position.

Worked as Assistant Manager of Hardy Shoe Store on Peachtree Street in downtown Atlanta.

1984

Son, John Nicklaus Pelt was born.

April 1985 – July 1991

2nd Pastorage - Served as Full-time Senior Pastor of Hill First Baptist Church; Athens, Georgia – The oldest African American Baptist Church in Athens.

> *"We praise God because He has done great things in our lives and in the works of the church. God deserves the praise for what has been accomplished for the past year. It is my intention to be led by Him and His Word.*
>
> *We, Pastor and Parishioners were united because of the will and power of God. I pray that we continue to be in tune with God's will because He does have the power to bring people together for the better.*
>
> *My family and I have thoroughly enjoyed our stay with you this year. We look forward to enjoying many more. May God's blessings be yours."* **(4/13/1986 1st Pastoral Anniversary Statement)**

While in Athens he served in numerous religious and social organizations to include:

- Northeast Baptist Ministerial Union where he served as President from 1987-1991;

- Metro Athens Ministerial Alliance where he served as President from 1990-1991;

- African American Fellowship;

- Northwest Baptist Sunday School Congress of Christian Education;

- City of Athens Library Board;

- Morning Optimist;

- Athens Pastoral Counseling Committee;

- OIC Board;

- People for People Organization;

- Lincoln Lodge No. 62, Prince Hall, Free and Accepted Masons.

During his tenure there, in 1987 he entered the Doctor of Ministry Program at Emory University/Candler School of Theology in Atlanta, Georgia.

"The most important reason I am applying for admission is because I have a zeal to obtain this degree. I am pursuing this advanced degree because I feel this is a part of my call to ministry. God has given me a zeal to study religion and the Christian Faith. I already have the required experience and educational background necessary for this endeavor. I have been active in ministry all of my adult life. For fourteen years I have been a proclaimer of the Gospel. My academic record reflects the seriousness with which I take my studies. In addition, I am applying for admission because I feel this degree will broaden my knowledge, skills and talents, thereby expanding my parish ministry. It will enable me to better serve in this and other areas of the ministry."

"After completion of this program, I plan to continue to work in parish ministry. In addition, I hope to become more involved in my local association and state and national

conventions. I plan to use my training and expertise to assist in developing programs of study for the local association of churches... I want to be a parish minister who has expertise in Christian Education, with emphasis on special seminar materials for the local church and association. I also look forward to presenting this special material in the state and national conventions." **(1987 Doctoral Application to Emory University)**

NOTE: He lived out/accomplished his goals presented in this application to Emory University's Doctoral Program. In his latter years, he regretted putting off the publication of the numerous seminars he developed and presented to various churches; associations, state and national conventions.

Awarded the Doctor of Ministry (DMin) Degree on May 11, 1992 from Emory University/Candler School of Theology. His dissertation was entitled: "Teaching Christian Fellowship in the Local Church: A Black Perspective"

July 1991 – October 2013

3rd Pastorage - Served as Full-time Senior Pastor of Liberty Baptist Church; Atlanta, GA. He was Liberty's ninth pastor.

During his tenure, he:

♦ Received numerous new and returning members;

♦ Reorganized the Sunday School, Wednesday Night Bible Study, and the Music, Trustee and Youth Ministries;

♦ Instituted a Sunday School Teacher's Certification Program and New Members Class;

- Established a Thursday Morning Bible Class for Seniors and a Saturday Bible Class emphasizing evangelism;

- Expanded the Homeless Ministry to include a time of prayer and worship and in later years partnered with Atlanta West Pentecostal Church of Lithia Springs, Georgia to further show Love in Action to those in need;

- Developed & conducted in depth training programs for the numerous ministers and deacons he ordained;

- Ordained the first female deacon in the history of Liberty;

- Organized a Ministry in Context Program to mentor Morehouse School of Religion students. Many of those ministers joined Liberty and served in various ministries while participating in the minister ordination program;

- Provided the leadership in creating the Praise Dance and Health & Wellness Ministries;

- Initiated an early morning worship service, Summer Enrichment and Community Outreach Program;

- For a season, hosted along with Deacon Bobby Strong, "Liberty Baptist Live" on AM 1480 WYZE Radio;

- Started an Open Forum and Leadership Council to keep the members informed;

During these years, Pastor Pelt was involved in several civic and religious organizations. They include:

- Atlanta Baptist Minister's Union (former President);

- Capital Ministries where he served as a board member of Holy Smoke;

- Concerned Black Clergy;

♦ Atlantans Building Leadership for Empowerment (ABLE);

♦ Habitat for Humanity where he worked in partnership with several other churches to build homes.

Local, State and National Associations & Convention involvements:

♦ Atlanta Baptist Association (former Moderator);

♦ An active member of the New Era Missionary Baptist Convention of Georgia, Inc. and the Progressive National Baptist Convention (PNBC).

♦ A lecturer on a variety of subjects at various local, state, regional and national associations and conventions.

♦ A PNBC Instructor of courses for Youth Ministers & Workers and Trustees.

♦ A New Era Missionary Baptist Convention of Georgia, Inc. Instructor of Baptist Doctrine and African American Worship in the Christian Church.

♦ 2nd and 1st Vice President & President (1998 – 2002) of the New Era Missionary Baptist Convention of Georgia, Inc. Congress of Christian Education. His leadership was instrumental in the successful transition of the annual Congress from Toccoa to the New Era Convention Center in Griffin.

"We are prayerful that God will speak to you afresh, as we convene here. The environment itself (the lake, trees, grass, birds, insects and open space) teaches us volumes concerning the handiwork of God. Furthermore, God has inspired and revealed new insights to our teaching staff. Therefore, we challenge you to be receptive to learning new truths. As a result, we are prayerful that you will be

strengthened, and that your work in the local Church will be reinforced.

May His ministry continue until His Kingdom comes to Earth as it is in Heaven." **(2002 Congress President Message)**

Service to Academic Community:

♦ **September 1992 – December 2011**: Adjunct Faculty member of the Interdenominational Theological Center (ITC) as an instructor of Baptist History and Polity at Morehouse School of Religion.

♦ President of the Morehouse School of Religion Alumni Association;

♦ Morehouse School of Religion Executive Board Member;

♦ Doctorate of Ministry (DMin) Mentor (Professor & Supervisor) in the Doctoral Program at United Theological Seminary of Dayton, Ohio from January 2003 – May 2008. Fourteen (14) students received Doctor of Ministry degrees under his leadership.

"As Mentor, I teach, guide, and supervise students throughout the 2 1/2-year program of study." **(2008 Clinical Pastoral Education (CPE) Application)**

A Pilgrimage to the Holy Land – Interdenominational Theological Center – Holy Land Pastoral Renewal Program

May 2 – 15, 2007 – The highlights of this trip were walking where Jesus walked, preaching in the City of Nazareth and being baptized in the Jordan River.

"We are doing well walking in the footsteps of Jesus. This has been a life changing experience." (2007 postcard sent to his wife Mary from Tiberias, Galilee)

Clinical Pastoral Education (CPE)

August 7, 2009 - Completed his sixth unit of CPE at Emory University Hospital Midtown and occasionally served as an "on call" Chaplain.

"Clinical Pastoral Education (CPE) is not required of me in my position as Senior Pastor. However, I feel led by the Spirit of God to become a Chaplain in an institution to some capacity. And to do so, I need at least one additional CPE unit. I completed one unit twenty years ago in Athens, Georgia. Therefore, I can say "yes" that I have taken CPE, but I cannot respond with clarity because of the time that has escaped since the training. However, I look forward to relearning many things that I have forgotten. I do know that CPE helps the student to face himself/herself; and in doing so he/she can help others face their issues." (2008 Clinical Pastoral Education (CPE) Application)

Liberty's New Church Building

As Liberty's Senior Pastor, his emphasis included practices to spread the Gospel of Jesus Christ in both conventional and innovative ways. As led by God, he was responsible for bringing forth the vision of building the new Liberty Church on its original site to accommodate the needs of a growing church and community.

"My family has grown spiritually during our tenure here. Mary is involved in the total ministry of the church. My sons

are active in their gifted areas. We have recently completed a new $2.5 million dollar facility. This building project stretched me to a new level of spiritual maturity because it was a very difficult process with many change orders and problems that were not easily or quickly resolved. I have learned many lessons from these experiences."

"The unique thing about my tenure at Liberty is the fact that I led this congregation through a very challenging building project. This campaign began in the mid-1990s and we moved into the facility in June of 2007. We demolished the old facility and rebuilt it in the same location in downtown Atlanta." **(2008 Clinical Pastoral Education (CPE) Application)**

Entrance Day for Liberty's new Sanctuary – June 17, 2007

April 9, 2006 was the original Entrance Date; then it was delayed to May 21, 2006; however, in accordance with God's perfect timing the actual Entrance Date was June 17, 2007 (Father's Day – exactly 34 years from the date of Pastor Pelt's initial sermon on June 17, 1973). The Dedication Day was July 15, 2007.

"Greetings!

We thank God for this greatly anticipated day. We thank all of you who have adjusted your schedules to be a part of this celebration. Your many prayers and words of encouragement have been the wind beneath our wings. Your presence makes our hearts glad.

Mary, I want you to know that I am deeply appreciative for the many years of wedded bliss. You are one in a million.

Tyrone and Nicklaus, keep working toward your goals. God has great things in store for you. You make me proud.

Liberty thank you for your love, respect and support. I am pleased to be your pastor and partner "at such a time as this." Let us keep praying that the spirit of Christ will continue to abide among us. Where the spirit of Christ is, there is liberty.

We praise God for the great things that He has done. To build a new church is more than an idea. It was no easy task. It was a remarkable venture into the unknown, into the darkness of human knowing. There were many traps, unannounced curves, unexpected roadblocks and oversized potholes that delayed and even sometimes attempted to stop the journey. However, with Jesus in front of us, and all around us, the journey was safe and the destination was sure.

This building project has been a revealing lesson in faith and determination. The key factor was to be willing to live through the uncertainties until God gave us a clear vision of our mission, and by my calculations this took a long time. During this process, I joined the prophet Habakkuk who asked, "Lord, how long?" The process was filled with many anxious days and sleepless nights. However, praise God, we stayed with it until God's revelation came.

When I was called to the church, I had hopes to renovate the present church and perhaps add an educational wing that is quite common to building projects. However, God did not want us to renovate our old structure or relocate to the suburbs as we considered, but build a new structure where we were.

To engage such a mammoth task required a special Word from the Lord, because the membership size was less than 350 even with the stretch of the imagination and the financial resources were limited for such a massive effort. Additionally, our church was in a neighborhood that had many social/economic challenges. This was a great struggle for me. From my deductions, relocation was the better option and renovation was the second, while rebuilding was the last. But God knows how to make the last first and the first last.

As the years passed and the events unfolded, God's vision was made plain to me. But before that happened, I was asking the same question that King Zedekiah asked, "Is there a word from the Lord?" I kept hearing the words of Booker T. Washington, "Cast down your bucket where you are." Of course, I wanted to hear a special scripture, or a special song; but as time passed, I became more convinced that God was calling us to fight the good fight of faith where we were. From that point forward, I could lead the congregation with a real sense of vision, confidence and conviction.

In reflecting over our journey, I can see how God has been good to us. We have encountered many of the problems that are common to the black church during building projects. We had a difficult time securing loans from the bank, as well as, many delays in getting the various building permits. The cost of the project escalated. Although we have had many meetings with the membership concerning the architectural design of the building, when the building started to take shape, several members had questions or concerns. Additionally, many thought that the sanctuary and rooms were going to be larger than they are. We have had our problems, but I have learned that God is a miracle worker and a problem solver.

It was God who brought us through the dark clouds of doubt and through the long nights of confusion. It was God who kept us and brought us to this pivotal point in our history. Therefore, we come to praise Him and thank Him "for a dream come true." "Had it not been for the Lord who was on our side, where would we be?" "Had it not been for the Lord who" united us and kept us, who guided us and led us, this day would have never come. Praise Him. Praise Him! Amen. Amen. Amen!

With Love,
J. Sherman Pelt, Senior Pastor
(2007 Entrance Day Souvenir Book-From the Pastor's Pen)

FINAL 5 YEARS

In spite of health challenges during the last 5 years of his life, Pastor Pelt remained an active, faithful and a willing vessel through whom God continued to minister to a world in need of salvation and hope.

November 2008

Diagnosed with Solitary Plasmacytoma - The type of cancer that usually precedes the bone cancer, Multiple Myeloma.

"When my physician called me that dark, chilly, rainy Tuesday night in my office, I was shocked to receive the news. For a few minutes after receiving the news, I probably

went through the typical swing of emotions, with the basic questions to follow ("Lord, why me;" "what am I going to do;" "how long will I live;" and etc.). In the rush of these ideas and emotions the text, "all things work together for the good" came to my mind, and it gave me a sense of calm in the storm. And it came to mind that I could use my struggle to give glory to God in ways I had not yet experienced by sharing this with others. Since that night, this text has been crystallizing in thoughts in regards to my personal grounding, and it is helping to shape the way I do ministry.

First, this Biblical idea is helping me to see that I am not cursed, nor am I hopeless. Life goes on and God is still moving and working in my life. Secondly, by having this condition and understanding it as I do, I am able to identify with the patients with a greater sensitive than ever before.

The thought of "all things working together," helps to shape a Pastoral Care approach that is broad enough to accept people at their point of suffering with a sense that they are still loved by God. This gives us a perspective of suffering that is more loving than what we find in the story of Job, as Job's friends pointed their finger and suggested that he was getting what he deserved for some unknown sin that he had committed. However, the "all things working together" concept provides a room that is large enough to embrace the person where he/she is without being judgmental.

As life proceeds down the road to the future, God is using all of our situations, and circumstances to produce a good result." (6/8/2009 Final Clinical Pastoral Education (CPE) Statement)

January 21, 2009

Sherman and I traveled by automobile to Washington, DC and was present as America's 44th President, Barack H. Obama took the oath of office.

November 2010

First stem cell transplant. Prior to this step in his treatment for this awful disease, he received radiation and chemotherapy medications. Just prior to the transplant he underwent an intensive chemotherapy regimen which caused him to be immunocompromised for an extended period of time requiring him to be isolated from public places. During this period of time he was required to have a full-time caregiver; therefore, I took a leave of absence from my job with the General Services Administration. During these intense three (3) months, daily visits to Northside Hospital's Blood and Marrow Transplant (BMT) Infusion Facility for treatments that lasted from 3-6 hours per day, seven days per week were required for the first 30 days. Thereafter, the number of days per week that treatment at the BMT Infusion Facility was required was reduced based on the lab results, to every other day, every three days, every week, etc. until day 100 after the transplant was reached. At any time during these 100 days, based on the lab results, the daily visits could be reinstated (this did happen).

February 27, 2011

Returned to the full-time pastorage of Liberty Baptist Church-Atlanta after a 3-month leave of absence and with the cancer in remission.

November 2012

Out of remission... the cancer returned.

June 17, 2013 (Father's Day)

Celebrated 40 years as a Gospel Preacher! 40 years exactly from June 17, 1973, the day he preached his initial sermon. Same text and subject – "The Prodigal Son"; Luke 15:11-32!

July 21, 2013

Final sermon preached at Liberty Baptist Church-Atlanta. "Preparing the Next Generation to Take the Lead"; II Timothy 3:14-15

Final written Sermon notes:

> *"Even though you are going to be leading the church during perilous times; difficult times; sick and sad times; carry the banner high and fight the good fight of faith...*
>
> *-Draw from what I taught you: vv. 10-12*
>
> *-Draw from your own life experiences: v. 14*
>
> *-Draw from the Scriptures: vv.15-17"*

July 2013

Second stem cell transplant at Northside Hospital. Again, I took a leave of absence to be my husband's full-time caregiver. My retirement was effective October 6, 2013.

Many times, over the years Pastor Pelt had been encouraged to become a published author; however, he did not seem to have the time to devote to it. During his Pastoral leave of absence for this, his 2nd stem cell transplant, he concluded to take the time to prepare many of the sermons, "Messages of Hope" he had preached over the years for publication. He also wanted to publish some of the "Food for Thought" teachable moments he shared with Liberty during 2013. In addition, he was also very excited about his autobiography, "The Journey of a Lifetime". From Day 2 or 3 after the transplant, every day he was typing on his iPad, in the car going to & from Northside Hospital and during his treatments, which lasted 3-6 hours/day.

At Northside Hospital's Blood & Marrow Transplant (BMT) Infusion Facility, he typed with such urgency that the medical personnel and fellow patients often asked him: "Pastor, what are you working on?" "Pastor, why are you working so hard?" "Pastor, take it easy; slow down; concentrate on your recovery." We did not know why he spent so much time typing every day during his treatment. We did not know why he typed with such urgency... now we know why – he had to get as must written as possible because his time was short on this earth.

September 15, 2013

22nd Anniversary as Senior Pastor of Liberty Baptist Church-Atlanta celebrated at Northside Hospital's BMT Infusion Facility, via Skype.

September 15, 2013

Final Family Picture.

October 6, 2013

Our final picture together.

October 8, 2013

Last day at home – we knew he would be admitted into Northside Hospital on this day; however, we did not know he would not return home alive again.

October 19, 2013

Requested that we (his wife and children) complete his book, "The Journey of a Lifetime."

October 25, 2013

Transferred to hospice in Stockbridge, Georgia.

October 31, 2013

Final visit by siblings.

October 31, 2013

Transition from earth to glory!

Exactly 45 years from the date his father was laid to rest at Oak Grove Cemetery in Clinton, Alabama

November 8, 2013

Last time back home (Riverdale, Georgia) and last time up the hill from our home (in honor of the many times Sherman and I walked up that hill on our many walks together) to begin the 250-mile trip back home to Boligee, Alabama.

Celebration of Life at Mt. Olive Baptist Church in Boligee, Alabama - the church where Sherman and I became husband and wife on August 19, 1978.

-Rev. Dr. Michael Neely Harris, Officiating – Pastor, Wheat Street Baptist Church; Atlanta, Georgia and Dr. Pelt's Pastor. Dr. & Mrs. Harris also visited our home and assisted with the final arrangements.

-Rev. Kewon M. Foster, Sr., Eulogist – Assistant Pastor, Liberty Baptist Church; Atlanta, Georgia (Liberty's 10th Pastor from February 2014 – December 2016) Rev. Foster also visited our home and assisted with the final arrangements.

November 9, 2013

Final Celebration of Life at Liberty Baptist Church; Atlanta, Georgia where Sherman served as Senior Pastor for 22 years.

-Rev. Dr. Michael Neely Harris, Officiating – Pastor, Wheat Street Baptist Church; Atlanta, Georgia and Dr. Pelt's Pastor.

-Rev. Kewon M. Foster, Sr., Eulogist – Assistant Pastor, Liberty Baptist Church; Atlanta, Georgia (Liberty's 10th Pastor)

-Entombment at Westview Cemetery Abbey; Atlanta, Georgia

Posthumous Recognition

Down through the years, Dr. Pelt received numerous honors, awards and recognitions. Posthumously his honors include:

-The renaming of the Liberty Baptist Church Christian Education Wing to **The J. Sherman Pelt Christian Educational Wing;**

-The naming of one of Atlanta's Meals on Wheels Routes to **The Dr. J. Sherman Pelt Meals on Wheels Route;**

-The receipt of The Gardner C. Taylor Preaching Award from the Morehouse School of Religion at The Interdenominational Theological Center.

When asked in 2002, "Is there a legacy that you would like to leave? His response was, *"I would like to be remembered as one who really cared for the people he served."*

I can hear his voice now repeating his favorite poem:

The Road Not Taken

Two roads diverged in a yellow wood,
And sorry I could not travel both
And be one traveler, long I stood
And looked down one as far as I could
To where it bent in the undergrowth;

Then took the other, as just as fair,
And having perhaps the better claim,
Because it was grassy and wanted wear;
Though as for that the passing there
Had worn them really about the same,

And both that morning equally lay
In leaves no step had trodden black.
Oh, I kept the first for another day!
Yet knowing how way leads on to way,
I doubted if I should ever come back.

I shall be telling this with a sigh
Somewhere ages and ages hence:
Two roads diverged in a wood, and I—
I took the one less traveled by,
And that has made all the difference.

--Robert Frost--

I have fought the good fight, I have finished the race, I have kept the faith. Finally, there is laid up for me the crown of righteousness, which the Lord, the righteous Judge, will give to me on that Day, and not to me only but also to all who have loved His appearing. II Timothy 4:7-8 KJV

Well done, good and faithful servant! (Matthew 25:23 KJV)

Pictorial Journey

A journey through highlights and fond moments of Dr. J. Sherman Pelt captured in photographs from the archives of Mary O. Pelt and M.O.P. Photography.

The photo on the back cover and obituary was taken by Mrs. Mary O. Pelt after worship at Liberty Baptist Church-Atlanta on Sunday, January 6, 2013.

The photo on the front cover was taken by Mrs. Mary O. Pelt on February 15, 2011 during a trip she and Dr. Pelt made to Savannah, Georgia. This trip took place two weeks prior to the end of his three month recuperation period after the first stem cell transplant.

GRANDPARENTS
Mr. & and Mrs. George & Lizzie Montgomery

PARENTS
Mr. & Mrs. John Sherman & Addie M. Pelt

Father and Son

John Sherman Pelt

School Days 1965—1966
Mount Hebron Elementary

Paramount High School - Boligee, AL
Class President - May 1974

SIBLINGS

Raymond, Fredrick, Sherman, Juanita, Nathaniel and George

George, Nathaniel, Sherman and Raymond
Pelt Family Reunion – July 3, 2011 – Atlanta, GA

George, Sherman, Raymond and Fredrick
Sherman's 50th Birthday Celebration – Atlanta, GA

Sherman and Juanita

Pelt Family Reunion – Mobile, AL – May 29, 2010
2nd Row: Sherman, George, Fredrick, Nathaniel, Raymond;
Front Row: Evonne & Juanita

DR. AND MRS. PELT (SHERMAN & MARY)

Wedding Photo at Mt. Olive Baptist Church – Boligee, AL
August 19, 1978

Wedding Photo Re-Shoot Session
August 1984

Liberty Baptist Church—Atlanta

30th Wedding Anniversary in Hawaii

Liberty Baptist Church—Atlanta

35th Wedding Anniversary
August 19, 2013

CHILDREN AND GRANDCHILDREN

Dr. and Mrs. Pelt and sons, Tyrone and Nicklaus

Dr. and Mrs. Pelt and sons, Tyrone and Nicklaus

Dr. Pelt and sons, Nicklaus (left) and Tyrone (right)

Dr. and Mrs. Pelt (center) and sons,
Nicklaus and his wife Chailoea (left) and Tyrone and his wife Cherline (right)

The only grandchild, Andrew, born during Dr. Pelt's lifetime

DR. J. SHERMAN PELT

Pastor & First Lady Pelt's return to Sunday Worship Services after first transplant where he performed the Baby Dedication of grandson, Andrew – February 27, 2011

Pastor Pelt with son, Tyrone and grandson, Andrew – March 6, 2011

Pastor Pelt with grandson, Andrew September 4, 2011

Pastor Pelt with Family
Son Nicklaus & daughter-in-law Chailoea (left), Mrs. Pelt (center),
son Tyrone & daughter-in-law Cherline (right) and grandson Andrew

Seated: Mrs. Pelt, Andrew, and Dr. Pelt
Standing: Tyrone, Cherline, Chailoea, and Nicklaus

Family Photo – December 31, 2018
Top: Tyrone, Mary, Christopher and Nicklaus
Bottom: Cherline, Amber, Andrew, Chailoea and Johnathan

Grandchildren: Siblings Amber and Andrew;
Siblings Christopher, Nolan and Johnathan
August 2020

CHURCHES

1ST PASTORAGE FROM MAY 1975 – AUGUST 1979

Pastor Pelt's 1st church, Bethlehem Baptist Church – Boligee, AL
He accepted this pastorage at the age of 20 and served here while attending college full-
time at Selma University and Livingston University (now the University of West Alabama).

2ND PASTORAGE FROM APRIL 1985 – JULY 1991

Pastor Pelt's 2nd church, Hill First Baptist Church – Athens, GA

Pastoral Installation, Hill First Baptist Church – Athens, GA
June 23, 1985

The First Family of Hill First Baptist Church – Athens, GA

Pastor Pelt in his office at Hill First Baptist Church – Athens, GA

Pastor Pelt preaching at Hill Frist Baptist Church – Athens, GA

Dr. J. Sherman Pelt with Rev. Finest Gandy, Mr. George Montgomery (Gramps),
Rev. Author Coleman (in rear) and Mr. Oscar Gandy.
Athens, GA

Mrs. Addie M. Pelt, Tyrone, Nicklaus and Mrs. Gertrude Gandy
Pastor Pelt's mother, sons, and Pastor Finest Gandy's wife

Pastor Pelt speaking at a program in observance of Dr. King's birthday.
January 21, 1988 – Athens, GA

3RD Pastorage from July 1991 – October 2013

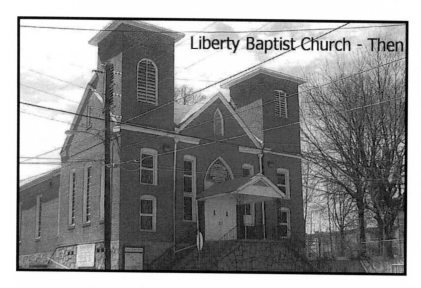

Historical photos of the Liberty Baptist Church—Atlanta

Liberty Baptist Installs New Pastor Sunday

Liberty Baptist Church, 395 Chamberlain Street, Atlanta, Georgia, will install its new Pastor, J. Sherman Pelt on Sunday, September 15, 1991 at 4:00.

Pastor Pelt, a native of Green County Alabama, formerly pastored at Bethlehem Baptist Church in Boligee, Alabama, and Hill First Baptist Church in Athens, Georgia.

He brings to Liberty a dynamic and fresh vision of the risen Christ. His commitment to the local church is reflected in his doctoral thesis "Teaching Christian Fellowship in the Local Church".

The Installation Service will be presided over by Dr. Charles J. Sargent, President New Era Missionary Baptist Convention, Dr. Michael Harris, Pastor of Wheat Street Baptist Church will deliver the sermon, and Liberty's Pastor Emeritus, Dr. Melvin Watson will present the mantel.

Other program participants and honorees will include local and state clergy, government officials, civic and community leaders.

The family of Liberty Baptist Church looks forward to this important service of installation. The public is Welcome. (pd.

INSTALLATION SERVICE

OF

Reverend J. Sherman Pelt

As Pastor of The

LIBERTY BAPTIST CHURCH
395 CHAMBERLAIN STREET, S.E.
ATLANTA, GEORGIA 30312

SUNDAY, SEPTEMBER 15, 1991

4:00 P.M.

Installation Program and newspaper announcement of the
Installation Service on September 15, 1991

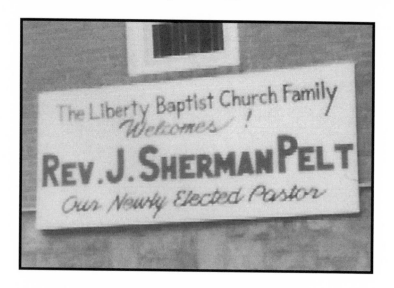

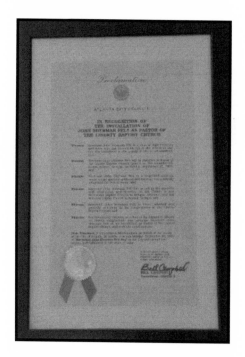

Atlanta City Council Proclamation of Pastoral Installation
Signed by Bill Campbell, Mayor of Atlanta

LIBERTY'S NEW BUILDING PROCESS

The Liberty Baptist Church–Atlanta building was demolished and reconstructed on the original site under the leadership of Dr. J. Sherman Pelt.

Early constructional rebuild of Liberty Baptist Church–Atlanta
(Dr. & Mrs. Pelt)

Constructional rebuild of Liberty Baptist Church–Atlanta.

Dr. Pelt at the site of the constructional rebuild of Liberty Baptist Church–Atlanta.

The new Liberty Baptist Church–Atlanta building completed under Dr. Pelt's leadership.

Ribbon cutting ceremony for the new Liberty Baptist Church–Atlanta building
Sunday, June 17, 2007

RELAXATION

Dr. Pelt enjoyed spending time with his family, reading, fishing, jogging, walking, gardening, grilling and traveling.

Dr. Pelt and Mrs. Pelt were blessed to travel to 44 of the 50 states.

Dr. Pelt's vegetable garden in Athens, GA

Dr. Pelt's large cabbage from his garden in Riverdale, GA

Dr. Pelt's BBQ wings were a favorite of his family and church family.

Dr. Pelt fishing in Boligee, AL – December 30, 2008

SPECIAL MEMORIES...

Preacher's License: St. Matthew Missionary Baptist Church – Eutaw, AL
August 12, 1973

Certificate of Ordination: St. Matthew Missionary Baptist Church – Eutaw, AL
August 8, 1975

Sherman and Mary
Graduation from Livingston University – 1979

Sherman and Mary
Graduation from Morehouse School of Religion at the
Interdenominational Theological Center – May 1983

Dr. Pelt and his mother, Mrs. Addie M. Pelt
Graduation from Emory University – May 1992

Doctoral Hooding by
Dr. Melvin H. Watson
May 12, 1992

Delivery of Commencement Address
Paramount High – Boligee, AL
May 23, 1996

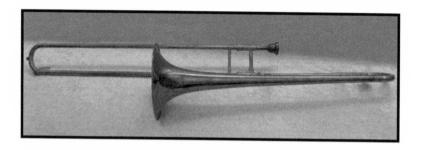

Dr. Pelt's instrument played in Paramount High School's Marching Band and
Selma University's Concert Band

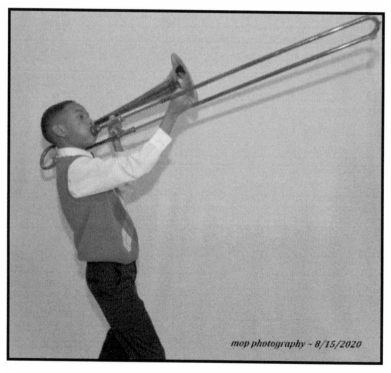

Dr. Pelt's grandson, Andrew, playing his trombone

Deacon George Montgomery (Gramps); Dr. J. Sherman Pelt; Rev. Finest Gandy
Pastor Pelt was licensed and ordained by Rev. Gandy

Dr. Pelt with his dear friend and classmate, Rev. Arthur Coleman, Sr.
at his 50th birthday celebration in Atlanta, GA

Brick on the campus of the University of West Alabama, formerly
Livingston University – Livingston, AL

Triplets!
Dr. Pelt's sons shaved their heads to match his new look after chemotherapy took his hair.
Tyrone (left) and Nicklaus (right)

Sherman & Mary's 39th High School Reunion -- at Paramount one last time!
God knew he would not be here for the 40th Reunion!
July 20, 2013 – Boligee, AL

Pelt Family Reunion & and Dr. Pelt's 58th Birthday
May 25, 2013 – Eutaw, AL

Inauguration of President Barack H. Obama
January 20, 2009 – Washington, D.C.

In the midst of history...
Dr. J. Sherman Pelt

Dressed for the cold weather on that historic day!
Dr. and Mrs. Pelt

Inauguration of President Barack H. Obama
January 20, 2009 – Washington, D.C.

Minister's Union, Atlanta Association & New Era

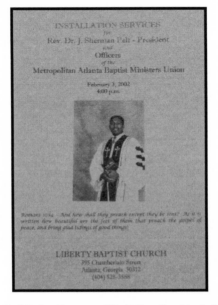

Installation Program of Dr. Pelt as President of
Metropolitan Atlanta Baptist Ministers Union

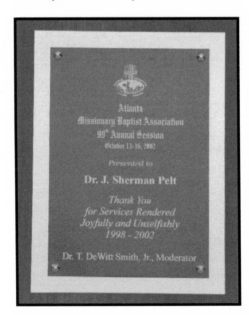

Award for Services rendered to the Atlanta Missionary Baptist Association

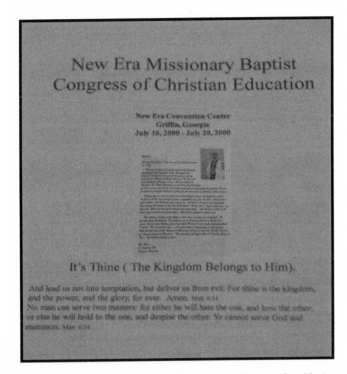

Congress Program during Dr. Pelt's tenure as Congress President

New Era Congress Tent – Griffin, Georgia
Dr. J. Sherman Pelt and Mary O. Pelt

Holy Land Pilgrimage - May 2 -15, 2007

"Words cannot express nor capture what I am experiencing right now."
"This has been a life changing experience."
(2007 Holy Land trip Dr. J. Sherman Pelt's handwritten notes)

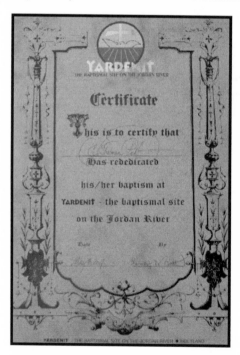

Jordan River Baptism Certificate – May 8, 2007

PUBLICATIONS

1992 Doctoral Dissertation
Teaching Christian Fellowship in the Local Church: A Black Perspective
Emory University – Candler School of Theology

Books drafted during his 2nd Stem Cell Transplant
"Messages of Hope", "Food for Thought", & and "The Journey of a Lifetime"
Finalized and published by his family.
(Available in paperback and ebook formats - www.peltfoundation.org)

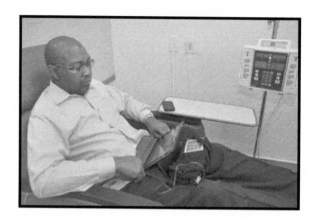

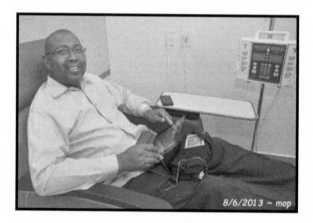

Working on "Messages of Hope", "Food for Thought" & "The Journey of a Lifetime"
During 2nd Stem Cell Transplant

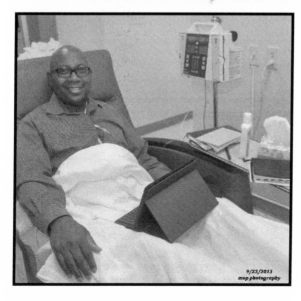

Rev. Dr. J. Sherman Pelt and First Lady, Mary O. Pelt
Celebrates 22nd Pastoral Anniversary at Liberty Baptist Church–Atlanta
on September 15, 2013 via Skype while at
Northside Hospital's Blood and Marrow Transplant Infusion Facility

FOREVER IN OUR HEARTS

Final photo with his family taken at his home – September 15, 2013
Top: Tyrone, Dr. Pelt, Andrew, Nicklaus; Lower: Mrs. Pelt, Cherline, Ozinnia, Chailoea

Final photo Dr. and Mrs. Pelt – October 6, 2013
Northside Hospital's Blood & Marrow Transplant Infusion Facility

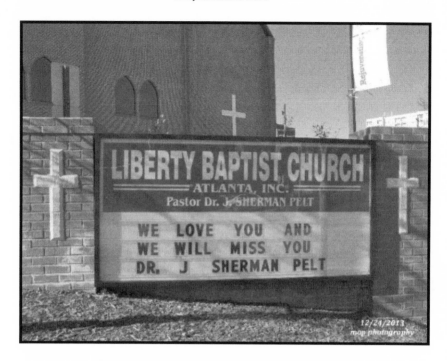

Celebration of Life Cover Photo taken by Mrs. Mary O. Pelt

Pelt Foundation

The Rev. Dr. J. Sherman Pelt Foundation, Inc., a non-profit corporation was established in 2014 to honor Dr. Pelt's life, ministry and legacy. This Foundation promotes Dr. Pelt's rich legacy of preaching, teaching and sharing the Good News of the Gospel, as well as, his passion for education, in general, and Christian Education, in particular.

The Pelt Foundation enthusiastically supports and promotes educational endeavors by providing scholarships to college and seminary students pursuing undergraduate and graduate degrees. As we assist in the creation of a brighter future for our scholarship recipients, the community of faith will be empowered through educational advancement. The Board of Directors and the Staff of the Pelt Foundation give praise to God for the opportunity to continue Dr. Pelt's legacy of generosity. God poured into him and he poured into others. His contributions are far reaching. To God be the glory for the tremendous difference he made in the countless lives he touched while on this earthly journey!

Please visit our website at: www.peltfoundation.org

"Everyone is called serve; young and old; rich and poor; male and female. Too often, we think that people of position and status should be served by others; when in fact great leaders are those servants/leaders who serve." - Rev. Dr. J. Sherman Pelt

Mail correspondences to:
The Rev. Dr. J. Sherman Pelt Foundation, Inc.
Post Office Box 161486
Atlanta, Georgia 30321

Phone:
(404) 600-1092

Email:
info@peltfoundation.org

Website:
peltfoundation.org